Classics 3S03

MW01253742

TABLE OF CONTENTS
& ACKNOWLEDGEMENTS

PAGE

Science or Morbid Curiosity?
The Casts of Giuseppe
Fiorelli and the Last Days
of Romantic Pompeii

Eugene Dwyer

W ITH THE WANING of the romantic movement in the second half of the nineteenth century, the feverish international interest that had focused on the Bay of Naples archaeological sites also appeared to dissipate. For a brief period in the 1860s imported cotton covered the fields lying above the unexcavated parts of Pompeii.[1] Fortuitously coincidental political and scientific developments, however, quickly returned the eyes of the world to Pompeii as a shocking new epoch of response to the discoveries began. In 1860, the newly created kingdom of Italy assumed the patrimony of the king of Naples and transformed a land that had languished for more than half a century. The agent of this larger change at Pompeii was Giuseppe Fiorelli, an energetic young man who had been imprisoned under the Bourbons but who in the new regime was appointed professor of archaeology at the University of Naples and director of museums and archaeological excavations in the new provinces of a united Italy.[2] Although Fiorelli already was a respected epigrapher and numismatist, his sensational 1863 invention of a method of casting the bodies of Pompeian victims carried his fame throughout Europe and America. But the fame of the casts and their creator came with a price, as they created their own moral dilemma for both excavators and visitors to the site.

Although previous attempts had been made to cast bodies from impressions left in the volcanic mud (fango), these new casts confronted the public with the agony of death, a sight that had been reserved only for the excavators themselves. All were taken aback by the grisly spectacle, but the response of both public and learned communities varied. In the mind of the scientifically inclined director, total disclosure was the best course even if some delicate sensibilities might be injured. Survivors of the recently ousted Bourbon regime, who might have been expected to entertain an opposing view, were silent in hopes of keeping their jobs. Foreigners, such as the recently arrived American consul in Naples, William Dean Howells, viewed the new discoveries in the broader context of contemporary events, which for Howells meant the modern horrors of the American Civil War. He saw four bodies in a city house restored as a temporary museum when he visited Pompeii in November 1864:

> You have read, no doubt, of their discovering, a year or two since, in making an excavation in a Pompeian street, the moulds of four human bodies, three women and a man, who fell down, blind and writhing, in the storm of fire eighteen hundred years ago; whose shape the settling and hardening ashes took; whose flesh wasted away, and whose bones lay there in the hollow of the matrix till the cunning of this time found them, and, pouring liquid plaster round the skeletons, clothed them with human form again, and drew them forth into the world once more. There are many things in Pompeii which bring back the gay life of the city, but nothing which so vividly reports the terrible manner of her death as these effigies of the creatures that actually shared it. The man in the last struggle has thrown himself upon his back, and taken his doom sturdily—there is a sublime calm in his rigid figure. The women lie upon their faces, their limbs tossed and distorted, their drapery tangled and heaped about them, and in every fibre you see how hard they died. One presses her face into her handkerchief to draw one last breath unmixed with scalding steam; another's arms are wildly thrown abroad to clutch at help; another's hand is appealingly raised, and on her slight fingers you see the silver hoops with which her poor dead vanity adorned them.
>
> The guide takes you aside from the street into the house where they lie and a dreadful shadow drops upon your heart as you enter their presence. Without, the hell-storms seem to fall again, and the whole sunny plain to be darkened with its ruin, the city to send up the tumult of her despair.
>
> What is there left in Pompeii to speak of after this? The long street of tombs outside the walls? Those that died before the city's burial seem to have scarcely a claim to the solemnity of death.[3]

Where the dead are concerned at Pompeii, compassion had at first been mixed with indifference, perhaps to be expected where the discovery of cadavers became routine. Responses to human remains at Pompeii begin with the first official, dispassionate notice of the discovery of a corpse: "A cadaver was discovered this morning, between the lapilli [the layer of pumice] and the soil, found together with eighteen bronze and one silver coin, which I am sending enclosed to the hands of Your Excellency."[4] As the official record of the excavation was a journal of expenses and receipts meant to justify the continuation of the efforts, the unprofitable human remains often assumed second place to more valuable finds. It did not take the excavators long, however, to observe that the discovery of a body often meant the discovery of coins, jewelry, or other treasure. Furthermore, philosophical contemplation of the dead amid the ruins of Pompeii had become a time-honored practice when the casting technique was perfected. There had even been a certain amount of stagecraft employed in the arrangement and display of skeletons to enhance this experience.[5] The discovery of the body of a person who had died a violent death held a certain thrill, all the more so if it belonged to a godless pagan. The casts made by Fiorelli instantly transformed public perception of the suffering of the Pompeians. Consequently, we must reflect on how the earlier presenters and consumers of the Pompeian experience conceived of the death and suffering of the victims. It can hardly be accidental that the period from the discovery of Pompeii to the perfection of Fiorelli's casting technique (about 120 years) coincided with the birth and death of romanticism and its replacement (or displacement) within the sphere of archaeology by a new scientific attitude.

Even before Fiorelli, the encounter with death was a memorable part of every tourist's experience of Pompeii, though it was usually mediated by art in the course of a promenade along the Street of the Tombs, with its ironic inscriptions and emblems of death or a visit to a subterranean cellar where a group of skeletons had once been found huddled together. The human imagination is ever active, and the public wanted to know what had happened in morbid detail. For those with a knowledge of classical languages, several passages in ancient literature conveyed some idea of the terrible experience of the victims of Vesuvius. Indeed, the population of Naples knew too much about sudden, catastrophic mortality brought about by disease or volcanic eruption. The city had been visited regularly by the plague and in the nineteenth century by cholera. An eruption of Vesuvius in 1631 killed at least four thousand in a few hours. During the worst of these periods of devastation the corpses literally piled up in the cemeteries. Terror interfered with the survivors' respect for the dead. The same saint, San Gennaro, who protected the Neapolitans from the plague and the volcano, on occasion withheld his protection. Such death was popularly viewed as divine retribution: "Naples sins, and Torre [del Greco] pays," was—and still is—commonly heard.[6] In the popular imagination, the Pompeians, known for their sybaritic lifestyle, deserved their fate. Pompeii and Herculaneum were a kind of Sodom and Gomorrah.[7] Even the man of science Stefano Delle Chiaje, who was the first to study the human remains of the Pompeians, believed their physiognomy showed evidence of a "relaxed and libidinous lifestyle."[8] If they had been Christian, things might have been different, but the treatment of human remains from Pompeii has had little or nothing in common with the treatment of remains from the Roman or Neapolitan catacombs.[9] Quite to the contrary, it might almost be said that Christians felt it their duty to display contempt for the victims' remains at Pompeii.[10]

Forensic interest in the bodies is noticeably lacking from the first official accounts, but some visitors had more curiosity about the circumstances of the victims' fate. As in many other aspects of Pompeian archaeology, Johann Joachim Winckelmann anticipated both the scientific method and the humane response of future generations of visitors. He did not know of any bodies found at either Pompeii or Herculaneum but only at Stabiae: "Three female bodies, one of which appeared to be the maid of the other two, and was carrying a wooden casket: this lay beside her, and had decomposed in the ash. The two other ladies both had golden bracelets and earrings, which were sent to the museum."[11] In Pompeii, though he did not find evidence of the bodies, he deduced from the locations of heavy items that these artifacts had been discarded as the flight of the inhabitants grew increasingly desperate.[12] Unfortunately, he gave no examples in support of this attractive theory, but it does suggest a human as well as an archaeological interest in the victims' plight.

Winckelmann's sympathy heralded a new era of interest in the human remains. The Stabian women observed by Winckelmann interested neither the authorities nor the learned Neapolitans charged with publishing the discovered treasures. As open-air excavation proceeded, however, the study of the archaeological context began to attract more attention, even while treasure hunting (collezionismo) continued to fund operations. In late 1766 the discovery of what was believed to be a military barracks at Pompeii produced a remarkable collection of arms, which eventually proved to be those of gladiators. The same building yielded thirty-four fugitives (fuggiaschi),

including some women laden with jewelry. One room housed an apparatus designed to hold ten prisoners by their legs; also found were four skeletons. Some at the time speculated that they were prisoners who had met their death in the stock, including Giovanni Battista Piranesi, who drew a sketch of the wretches held by their legs with a row of skulls looking down on them from a shelf at the back of the room [FIG. 1].[13] Significantly, in the twelve or so years between the discovery of the room and Piranesi's drawing, several dramatic discoveries compelled people to focus on the archaeological context of the fate of the victims as a novel, and perhaps defining, feature of the Pompeian excavations.[14]

The Austrian emperor Joseph II, brother of Queen Maria Carolina of Naples, was a notable beneficiary of Winckelmann's teachings. On a visit to Pompeii in 1768 Joseph was taken to a subterranean room in the structure that became known as the House of the Emperor Joseph II. There he and the rest of the party saw an intact skeleton, presumably of a victim who had perished in that place. Egon Cesar Conte Corti, referring to Joseph's correspondence with the empress Maria Theresa, noted that "for a long time the Emperor stood reflectively before these tokens of an intense human drama."[15]

This imperial tableau vivant attained symbolic status and it was re-created on numerous occasions with different participants. Several years later Pierre Jacques Onésme Bergeret de Grancourt together with his party, including the painter Jean-Honoré Fragonard, visited the same place. In his journal Bergeret noted that "in one house, among others, in the room downstairs where they must have done the washing, we could see all the implements, the stove, the washtub, etc....and a heap of volcanic ash upon which rested the skeleton of a woman, as if, having tried to escape from the choking ashes coming in from all sides, she had finally fallen backwards and died. Everything about the placement and position of her bones indicated that this was clearly what had happened, and one remains stunned at the contemplation of the events of 1,700 years ago."[16] A drawing by Fragonard recorded a virtual replay of the same scene as witnessed by a French party, including Abbé de Saint-Non, as published in the latter's *Voyage pittoresque* in 1781 [FIG. 2], a choice that demonstrates how the remains had gained a status equal to the antiquities.[17]

Between 1771 and 1774, the center of attention at Pompeii was the villa suburbana, thought to belong to Arrius Diomedes, whose name was known from an adjacent

FIGURE 1
Giovanni Battista Piranesi (Italian, 1720–1778), *Prisoners in the Barracks of the Gladiators at Pompeii*, ca. 1778. Pen and brush and blackish-brown ink on paper, squared in black chalk. Kupferstichkabinett. Staatliche Museen zu Berlin, Berlin, Germany.

Photo: Bildarchiv Preussischer Kulturbesitz/Art Resource, NY.

FIGURE 2
Jean-Honoré Fragonard (French, 1732–1806), *Travelers Viewing a Skeleton at Pompeii*, 1775. From Jean Claude Richard de Saint-Non, *Voyage pittoresque, ou description des royaumes de Naples et de Sicile* (1781). Los Angeles, Research Library, Getty Research Institute, DG821.S14 1781.

monument on the Street of the Tombs. Excavations in the cellar had revealed a grisly sight: twenty or so women and children "of whose flesh there remained nothing but an impression in the earth, with the bones fallen into disorder, the hair partly preserved around some of the heads, and [even] some of the plaited tresses. Of their clothing there was nothing but ashes to be found, but these preserved the texture of the material which had surrounded their forms, permitting one to distinguish very clearly the fineness of the weave and the weight of the fabric."[18] The director of the excavations, Francesco La Vega, sent sixteen pieces cut from the volcanic impressions to the museum "in order to give evidence."[19]

When F. P. Latapie toured the villa in 1776 the bones had been laid out on tables and were gradually disappearing as successive visitors came through. He admitted to having taken for his personal museum "a bone more than seventeen centuries old."[20] Charles Dupaty, who saw the impressions in the museum at Portici, wrote: "One [impression] represents half of her bosom, which is of exquisite beauty; another a shoulder, a third a portion of her shape, and all concur in revealing to us that this woman was young, and that she was tall and well made, and even that she had escaped in her shift; for some pieces of linen are still adhering to the ashes."[21] This last observation of Dupaty's was to prove helpful to the woman's—and, indeed, all the Pompeians'—reputations and comforting to a subsequent, more prudish generation.

Seventy years later Charles Dickens responded viscerally to the Bay of Naples, in particular to the residual sense of death that still hung about Pompeii: "In the cellar of Diomede's house, where certain skeletons were found huddled together, close to the door, the impressions of their bodies on the ashes, hardened with the ashes, and became stamped and fixed there, after they had shrunk, inside, to scanty bones."[22] His success in reconstructing the progress of the destruction surpassed that of most visitors: "Nothing is more impressive and terrible than the many evidences of the searching nature of the ashes, as bespeaking their irresistible power, and the impossibility of escaping them. In the wine cellars, they forced their way into the earthen vessels: displacing the wine, and choking them, to the brim, with dust. In the tombs, they forced the ashes of the dead from the funeral urns, and rained new ruin even into them. The mouths, and eyes, and skulls of all the skeletons, were stuffed with this terrible hail."[23]

Dickens must be placed among the romantic visitors to Pompeii for his imaginative reconstruction of the terrible fate suffered by the ancient Pompeians. For one, the impressions of the bodies, or what could be conserved of them, had been removed first to Portici and then to the Real museo borbonico in Naples long before Dickens saw them. He might, in fact, have seen them in the latter place and restored them to their original context as an act of artistic license, or he might have borrowed the observation from contemporary tour guides. One detail that stands out is the tendency of the fine volcanic ash to penetrate virtually every cavity in the ruins. This phenomenon had long been noted, especially in the cellar of the Villa of Diomedes, where the skeletons mentioned by Dickens had been found. So completely had the ashes penetrated this space that the excavator, La Vega, believed they had arrived in liquid form. Others had even gone so far as to argue that a flood, and not a volcanic eruption, had destroyed Pompeii. A contemporary scientific report, however, contradicts Dickens's morbid but compelling assertion that the victims had been invasively violated by the insidious ash. In an 1854 study the pathologist Stefano Delle Chiaje found only one skeleton among the seventy-odd examples that he collected with ash from the eruption within the cranial cavity. There can be little doubt that Dickens invented or exaggerated this memorable detail to re-create the disaster according to his romantic fantasy.[24]

Pity for the victims emerges as a recurring theme among visitors' accounts from the 1780s onward. For example, Dupaty described a scene that is all too familiar to students of Pompeii: "But what do I perceive in that chamber. They are ten deaths heads. The unfortunate wretches saved themselves here, where they could not be saved. This is the head of a little child: its father and mother then are there! Let us go up stairs again; the heart feels not at ease here."[25]

On May 12, 1812, an excavation in the Street of the Tombs produced a piteous spectacle: a woman and three children were uncovered in the vicinity of the Mammia hemicycle. The architect Carlo Bonucci supplied the following analysis of the scene in his popular guide of the 1820s:

> Vesuvius had for an instant suspended his fury, when an unfortunate mother bearing an infant in her arms, and with two young daughters, endeavoured to profit by the opportunity, and to fly from their country-house to Nola, the city least threatened by this unspeakable catastrophe! Arrived at the foot of [the Mammia hemicycle], the volcano recommenced its ravages with redoubled fury. Stones, cinders, fire, melted and boiling substances, rained from all sides, and surrounded the miserable fugitives. The unfortunates sought refuge at the foot of a tomb, where reposed perhaps the ashes of their fathers; and invoking in the most frightful despair the gods, deaf to their prayers, they closely embraced their mother as they breathed out their last sigh, and in this situation they remained.[26]

Bonucci explained the victims' arrival at the Mammia tomb as an interruption in their futile attempt to flee from a country house to the city due north of Pompeii, which was known to have escaped the fury of the eruption. Unfortunately, as Bonucci and his audience knew, such a flight would have taken the mother and her children even closer to Vesuvius and was therefore doomed to end in failure, which only added to the poignancy of this scene.

Joseph Franque selected the subject of the mother and her children for his large history painting *Scene during the Eruption of Vesuvius* [see p. 161, FIG. 3]. Standing in the remains of their chariot, the figures embrace at the moment they are overcome by the irresistible volcanic surge. Dressed in loosely flowing and revealing garments, the mother and her children recall the Vatican sculpture of Laocoon and his sons as they succumb to their fate. The pathos and beauty of their delicate and shapely limbs and the sensitive, terrified expressions on their faces elicit both admiration and pity from the viewer.

Thanks to the popularity of Bonucci's guide and Franque's painting, the mother and her children became an established icon in Pompeian lore prefiguring Fiorelli's sensational casts. Thomas Gray wrote the same victim into his 1830 novel, *The Vestal*, as the character Favilla:

> "I can go no farther," said she. "Kiss me and leave me, my children." With one voice they declared that her fate should be theirs.... She was just able to reach the hemicycle on the left hand, near the gate, when she sank exhausted. Her daughters knelt beside her, and she threw her arms around them and blessed them. Faithfully did these girls redeem their promise to save her or to die with her. From that embrace

they rose not. The thick falling ashes closed over them, as the waves of the sea close over their victims.[27]

Gray, like Edward Bulwer-Lytton after him, introduced Christian morality into the lives of his heroes, thus separating them from the rest of the decadent Pompeians, who, the reader must suppose, deserved their fate. In the course of his novel he made use of the notorious sexual emblems found in Pompeii to indicate widespread moral depravity. He was heartened, however, by Dupaty's observation that the women in the cellar of the villa suburbana were clothed, thus refuting the opinion of some that the fugitives had fled "almost naked."[28]

Gray's pioneering use of the new archaeological context to reconstruct the last moments of the victims' lives anticipated the technique of Bulwer-Lytton's *Last Days of Pompeii* (1834). Through this popular novel, which fused archaeology and fiction, a worldwide audience became familiar with the Temple of Isis, the House of the Tragic Poet, the House of Pansa, the villa suburbana of Arrius Diomedes, and other stops on the Pompeian itinerary of the day, and they also read plausible explanations of the deaths of certain victims.

Appreciation of Pompeii usually required the visitor to look beyond the horror of the destruction to see beauty amid death. Bulwer-Lytton was able to achieve this necessary quality of good fiction by coloring in features not present in the archaeological record and sometimes going well beyond the outlines of the historical evidence. By Bulwer-Lytton's time, it was well known that many fleeing victims carried lamps or lanterns, presumably to help them find their way in the ash-darkened streets.[29] Bulwer-Lytton's invention of the blind girl, Nydia, who alone was able to guide her companions through the confusion, was a brilliant way to extricate his heroes from the dying city—but, unlike Franque's pictorial and Gray's fictional depiction of the mother who perished with her children at the Mammia sepulcher, Bulwer-Lytton's invention had no supporting archaeological evidence.

In the wake of Bulwer-Lytton, Ferdinand Gregorovius composed *Euphorion* (1858), a long narrative poem in German hexameters about the escape from disaster and at the same time from slavery by a fictional Pompeian Greek artist.[30] Although for the most part he was faithful to the archaeological record in his tale, Gregorovius concentrated more on the art of Pompeii than on the death of its inhabitants. But he soon became a convert to the new science. In August 1864, between the publication of the first and second editions of *Euphorion*, Gregorovius viewed the casts of the victims in the presence of Fiorelli. He was moved in particular by the fate of "the young girl, who, in despair, has lain down to sleep the sleep of death; the figure as graceful as that of a slumbering Hermaphrodite."[31] In response, he added a note to the 1884 edition concerning the new casts, calling them examples of "life incarnate in its most awful tragedy" and "most noteworthy of all statues." He added, "what once only the fantasy of the poet might have conjured up, he [now] has in full-blown reality in front of him, and as evidence of the moment itself."[32]

The confusion of pity, vulnerability, and erotic attraction is a familiar topos in nineteenth-century art and literature.[33] A prominent Pompeian example of this phenomenon was Théophile Gautier's resurrection of the famously admired young woman from the cellars of the villa suburbana as femme fatale in his Pompeian novel *Arria Marcella*, published in 1852.[34] Enchanted by the sight of the impressions in the Real museo borbonico, Gautier's hero Octavian embarks on an adventure that eventually leads to a tryst with the spirit of the dead woman. As Octavian and the dead woman are on the verge of fulfilling their desires, the sudden arrival of Arria's father, who has just embraced Christianity and now condemns his daughter's pagan sensuality, interrupts the scene. To Gautier, the Pompeians represented an exotic, eroticized antiquity not far removed from its contemporary equivalent, the Orient, which would become more immediately accessible through Fiorelli's casts.

Gautier's fantasy derived from an object exhibited in the Naples museum, which had been admired by many before him, and an erotic element had always been implicit in the making and exhibiting of the plaster casts of victims. This element of sexual fantasy had been present, if in more conventional form, since the discovery of the first female body impressions. The impressions from the Villa of Diomedes can be considered the beginning of a romantic quest to recover lost beauty. After their removal to the museum and the discovery of the mother and her children at the Mammia tomb, an attempt was made to cast the body of a woman found in the atrium of the House of the Faun in March 1831. This unfortunate person had dropped and scattered the collection of gold jewelry she had been carrying and sought refuge in one of the rooms surrounding the atrium. The position of her body showed her frantic effort to protect herself from the collapsing ceiling. The traces of her fine clothing were clearly visible in the ash that had solidified around her. But what caught the attention of the excavators was the impression of her beautiful foot and elegant sandal. Unfortunately efforts to make a cast of her body were unsuccessful.[35] Gautier's imaginative fantasy was, nevertheless, the fictional analogue to an actual archaeological effort.

This survey brings us to 1863, when Fiorelli made his epoch-making casts. Although plaster of paris had been used previously to cast wooden objects such as cabinets and doors, and even parts of cadavers, a casting of a complete body had never been attempted. By ordering his workers to stop digging and to inform him at the first appearance of a cavity in the fango, Fiorelli set the stage for a dramatic new discovery.[36] He lost no time in displaying his casts to the visitors who flocked to Pompeii in the 1860s in response to the news of his discovery. With the exhibition of plaster casts of victims in their death throes, a new element of shock was added to the experience of the visit. For the most part, the public responded positively to Fiorelli's casts [FIG. 3], and the exhibition played a critical part in Fiorelli's plan to finance the excavations by charging an admission fee.[37]

Most visitors and scholars regarded the innovation as positive and did not object much to the exhibition of the casts.[38] A typical reaction was that of the archaeologist Heinrich Brunn, who praised Fiorelli's ingenious discovery and published a careful description of the excavation in the *Bullettino della corrispondenza archeologica* for May–June 1863. Brunn admired the casts for the clarity of the bodily forms and the "artistic beauty of the figures themselves." The aesthetic, sculptural qualities of the casts were widely appreciated, and the sculptor Tito Angelini petitioned to have the admission fee waived while he transformed two bodies, a mother and her daughter [FIG. 4], into a work of art.[39]

Brunn further noted that the nudity to which students of ancient civilization had become accustomed in art was not found in real life, "vita stessa degli antichi." The inhabitants of ancient Pompeii were, in fact, clothed no more scantily than the modern Neapolitans, though the clothing worn by the Pompeian victims had lost its normal contours in the fango. But the evidence suggested that both men and women wore trousers. One of the women wore a scarf "all'uso degli orientali."[40]

FIGURE 3
Giacomo Brogi (Italian 1822–1881). *Interior of the Pompeii Museum.* Photograph. Private collection.

Photo: Courtesy Eugene Dwyer.

FIGURE 4
Giorgio Sommer (German, 1834–1914), *Cast of a Mother and Daughter.* Photograph. Private collection.

Photo: Courtesy Eugene Dwyer.

FIGURE 5
Cast of a Man. Photograph. Private collection.

Photo: Courtesy Eugene Dwyer.

This moral rehabilitation of the ancient Pompeians suited the program of the new archaeologists. The fact that the ancients wore pants [FIG. 5] was a detail of exaggerated importance. Before Fiorelli's discovery, the wearing of trousers had been thought to distinguish the moderns from the ancients—not simply in the trousers' practicality but also in the greater degree of modesty they afforded. Transported back into ancient times, Gautier's Octavian was a ridiculous sight in his frock coat and trousers. The new archaeological evidence contrasted with the picture of ancient dress gleaned from Pompeian paintings. Even while the heavily clothed Pompeian victims were being uncovered, Hippolyte Taine was writing of the Naples frescoes: "The painters of these pictures enjoyed a unique advantage, one which no others have possessed, even those of the Renaissance, of living amid congenial social customs, of constantly seeing figures naked and draped in the amphitheater and in the baths, and besides this, of cultivating the corporeal endowments of strength and fleetness of foot. They alluded to fine breasts, well-set necks, and muscular arms as we of the present day do to expressive countenances and well-cut pantaloons."[41]

Ironically, Taine based his vision of ancient dress on a vision of ancient life that was relatively new to Europeans, having been revealed and promulgated through the publication of the Pompeian and Herculanean frescoes only a century before.[42] This view of antiquity represented contemporary European social currents and a desire for freedom and erotic license more than the ancient reality. Brunn and his colleagues, representing the new spirit of scientific archaeology, gave the lie to the claimed archaeological correctness of neoclassicism and asserted that the evidence now proved this vision wrong. The dream of antiquity was now shown to be just that—a dream. Yet dreams, especially dreams based on aspirations of freedom, die hard. The rejection of an erotically charged vision of the antique in favor of a banal realism required the sacrifice of many cherished ideas about the ancients. The ghosts of the morally debased, pagan Pompeians had always enjoyed a certain celebrity.

Fiorelli, the pioneer in exhibiting physical human remains to the public, was also the pioneer in demonstrating this new morality. Not surprisingly he deliberately reversed the Bourbon policy in each area. While the rejection of neoclassical fashion was part of a general change in European taste following the fall of Napoleon, the Neapolitan reaction was specifically linked to the political events in Naples under the Bourbon restoration.[43] The reign of the scholarly but pious Francis I (1825–30) brought mixed fortune for antiquities. Francis actively supported the museum and the excavations at Pompeii, and he encouraged the resumption of excavations at Herculaneum. But his religious zeal and the need to reassert his control over his possessions led him to order strictures concerning the museum's collection of erotic artifacts. Even before his accession, he had suggested in 1819 that all obscene items in the museum's collections be kept in a closed room, to be known as the Cabinet of Obscene Objects (Gabinetto degli oggetti osceni), with admission limited to "persons of mature age and established morals."[44] In 1823 the name was changed to the less provocative Cabinet of Reserved Objects (Gabinetto degli oggetti riservati), with admission only by permission of the king. Many visitors of the time agreed with the morally conservative monarch in expressing their distaste for erotic Pompeii, no doubt in reaction to excesses of the Napoleonic period. Others were interested in Pompeian culture but preferred to veil this interest in conventional morality by condemning the manners of the Pompeians when the opportunity presented itself.

Many Neapolitans and visitors, however, harbored republican ideals, and these ideals were closely associated with the unique archaeological patrimony of the region. In 1848 political events gave Neapolitan liberals the opportunity to establish a constitution limiting royal power. Some liberal party members immediately challenged the status of the museum—then known as the Real museo borbonico—as the repository of the inherited wealth of King Ferdinand II. They argued that material from the archaeological sites belonged to the kingdom, not to the king. The constitutional program, containing a lengthy proposal for the reorganization of the Naples museum, was largely the work of Fiorelli.[45] Under Fiorelli's plan the pornographic objects were to remain closed to girls and boys, but women might view them with permission of the superintendent.[46] The proposal also called for the establishment of a museum at Pompeii intended to hold, in addition to artifacts of various common types, "human and animal skeletons."[47] This plan, however, came to nothing because the constitutional government failed and the king regained power. In addition to rejecting the planned reorganization of the museum, the king rebuffed a further proposal of Fiorelli's to send the human remains from Pompeii to the Istituto di anatomia of the University of

Naples.[48] Even more publicly, Ferdinand demonstrated his regained power by tightening his hold on the Cabinet of Reserved Objects. In 1849, in response to the failed attempt to establish a constitution and in anticipation of Pope Pius IX's visit to Naples, "the religious hypocrisy of government agents provoked strict orders that the door of this collection be closed and riveted, and all the Venuses and other painted and sculpted nudes, regardless of artist, be withdrawn from public view."[49]

The pope's arrival in Neapolitan territory and his reception by the devout King Ferdinand was celebrated as a triumph of Catholicism, and the political barometer of the Cabinet of Reserved Objects sank to its lowest register as once again the depravity of the Pompeians offered a suitable foil for the demons of contemporary politics. On the occasion of an elaborately staged visit to Pompeii on October 22, 1849, the pope blessed the people assembled in the amphitheater, and according to Stanislas d'Aloe, "his blessing served as well to sanctify that place so brutally profaned by the bloody spectacles of the ancients." Not only the amphitheater but also the forum and the temples of the gods were considered by d'Aloe as "place[s] profaned by the idolatry and by the depravity of the ancient inhabitants."[50] In a florid commemorative inscription written for this occasion, the learned Abate Gaetano Leofreddi likewise referred to the city's ruined monuments as "evidence of divine vengeance" ("ultionis divinae vestigia") and made an explicit comparison between ancient depravity and modern revolution.[51] Further suppression of the pornographic collection followed in 1852 and 1856, the last possibly in pious reaction to the cholera epidemic of 1855.

The scholarly, positivist attitude of Fiorelli toward human behavior and human remains firmly opposed the religious and moralizing perspective of many of his contemporaries.[52] Nevertheless, despite attempts to prevent it, a republican spirit and a scientific attitude toward the ancients eventually won out over "religious hypocrisy" (to use Fiorelli's term). With the victory of Giuseppe Garibaldi and the abdication of the Bourbon dynasty, the fortunes of the pornographic collection rose immediately. By a proclamation of Garibaldi, the collection was reopened on September 18, 1860, and under Fiorelli's supervision, a scholarly catalogue was prepared for publication in 1866. Women and boys, "uomini di fresca età," were still not permitted to view the objects, according to Raffaele Gargiulo's 1864 guidebook, though access was otherwise much freer than under the previous regime.[53]

As I have noted, the period from the discovery of Pompeii to the perfection of Fiorelli's casting technique coincided with romanticism and its replacement within the sphere of archaeology by a new scientific attitude. By a fortunate coincidence the latter part of this change in historical mentality fell directly within the life experience of a prominent archaeologist of the age, Charles Ernest Beulé. In his *Drame du Vesuve* of 1872 Beulé summed up a lifetime of experiencing Pompeii:

> The burial of five towns by Vesuvius is a proper drama to strike the imagination. Some poetic details have been added; the subject is fit for a novel. Bulwer draped it in his color. Today the prejudices have taken root, the errors have become popular.
>
> As a youth I experienced in their simplicity the delights of a sudden intimacy with antiquity. Later, after a period of four years in Greece, I found Pompeii small and its art seemed to me that which it is—an art of decadence. Finally, having arrived at mature age, I sought the explanation of extraordinary occurrences for which I, like so many others, had accepted banal explanations. I realized that the truth has more charm than convention and that the strongest poetry is the poetry of facts.

11

That which the ignorant call a wonder is nothing but a natural phenomenon for science. I wanted to account for the circumstances of this phenomenon. Vesuvius is the author of disasters that one believes are without precedent. I have conducted my inquiry with the patience of a magistrate who prepares a case and follows the clues of a crime: these are the results of the investigation which I lay before the judgement of the public.[54]

True to his promise, Beulé gave a meticulous description of the four bodies cast by Fiorelli in 1863. He began with the woman who had fallen on her back [FIG. 6]. Although her features were indistinct, she had obviously died of suffocation. She strained her head upward to breathe the air, supporting herself with her right hand, while she drove off an invisible foe with her left.[55] Her hair was wrapped about her head in a crown. Her chest was flattened and her breasts compressed under the weight of the soil. The sleeves of her tunic were harmoniously curved, but the glass-paste buttons that held them had deteriorated. In her flight she had gathered up her skirts about her hips, so that she appeared pregnant. Her thighs were covered by a fine garment like a slip, similar to those that had been noted in the impressions of the villa suburbana. Such a garment was intended to protect the dignity of the wearer from accidental gusts of wind. Ancient sculptors usually ignored such garments, though soldiers on the Column of Trajan wore them. In Pompeii even slaves and women of the people wore them. In conclusion, Beulé wrote, the woman was "grand, elegant, with a leg '*bien prise et charmente*,' and a foot '*admirablement cambré*.'" This last was well covered to protect her from the hot cinders over which she had to flee. She wore a silver ring and gold earrings. She carried a silver mirror and a miniature amber statuette of Amor. From these curious treasures, and from the proximity to the place where the body was found, Beulé suggested that this woman—whose fine clothing and treasures were inconsistent with the humble quarter—might have been a prostitute. "The evidence is slight; let us leave in peace not their bodies, which we must examine forever, but their memory." Austen Henry Layard, who examined her no less carefully, identified her as a housewife on the strength of the iron key she had with her. Yet here too the writer's eye for beauty prevails. "Her garments are gathered up on one side, leaving exposed a limb of beautiful shape. So perfect a mould of it has been formed by the soft and yielding mud, that the cast would seem to be taken from an exquisite work of Greek art."

FIGURE 6
Giorgio Sommer (German, 1834–1914). *Cast of a Pregnant Woman.* Photograph. Private collection.

Photo: Courtesy Eugene Dwyer.

FIGURE 7
Cast of a Young Woman. From an album of photographs of Pompeii by various artists, 1870–82. Los Angeles, Research Library, Getty Research Institute, 89.R.14 (8).

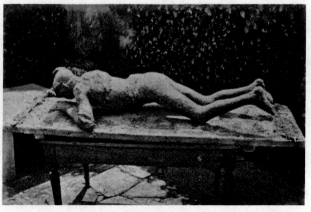

The woman, most often identified in the guidebooks and on photographs as "the pregnant woman," remained at the center of attention at Pompeii until 1875, when a still more beautiful woman was successfully cast [FIG. 7].[56] From that day until the present, the woman of 1875 has continued to be celebrated—most recently by Yusef Komunyakaa.[57] Fiorelli's "pregnant woman," however, has disappeared without trace —proving, perhaps, that novelty and physical beauty were the keys to the casts' popularity.[58]

The advent of the casts marked a new era in the history of interpretation of Pompeii. The innovation coincided with the Risorgimento, which brought freedom from certain kinds of religious oppression to Naples and Pompeii. A new spirit in archaeology suited the change in government, in which, as Beulé wrote, the poesy of facts eclipsed that of the imagination. Even during the earlier, romantic period the novelists were beholden to archaeologists such as Andrea de Jorio and Carlo Bonucci for their information. After Fiorelli, however, materialist history came to monopolize the Pompeian discourse. Gregorovius bore witness to this change in his testimony to the evocative power of the casts. Popular literature saw Bulwer-Lytton and Gautier give way to Overbeck and Mau.[59] In the graphic arts, photography, which replaced engraving, suited the historians more than the novelists. But even as the characteristic image of the Pompeian victims shifted from half-nude to trousered men and women, pity and Eros remained constant sentiments in the hearts of the viewers. And the viewers in both periods were assumed for the most part to be male, although the American Thomas Gray and the Englishman Bulwer-Lytton wrote for a more gender-balanced audience. Both the old and new periods witnessed horrified shock among some viewers. Dupaty and Piranesi conveyed their dismayed response at an early date, but in 1847 Luigi Settembrini gave this discomfort its most compelling expression: "But now you, my friend Fiorelli, have discovered human pain, and whoever is human can feel it."[60] In the end, the question—still unresolved—lies in the decision to study or to bury the victims.[61]

Notes

[1] William Dean Howells, *Italian Journeys* (1867; Marlboro, Vt., 1988), 57–68, esp. 61.

[2] On the life and career of Giuseppe Fiorelli, see G. Kannès, "Fiorelli, Giuseppe," in *Dizionario biografico degli Italiani* (Rome, 1997), 48:137–42.

[3] Howells 1988 (note 1), 67. When William Dean Howells saw them, they were exhibited in the House of the Skeletons (VI, Ins. Occ., 27: Casa degli scheletri or Casa dei cadaveri di gesso). Hence, his reference to the Street of the Tombs, which began nearby, is topographical as well as topical.

[4] Giuseppe Fiorelli, *Pompeianarum antiquitatum historia* (Naples, 1860), 1:2 (April 19, 1748). The body was probably that of a fugitive (*fuggiasco*), who had begun his flight after the rain of pumice (lapilli) had stopped and before the surges that followed the pumice. The word "soil" (*tierra*) here probably indicates not the ancient ground level but the modern cultivated surface.

[5] I have in mind the skeleton displayed in a lower room of the House of the Emperor Joseph II. I am not aware of any outright falsification of evidence of human remains.

[6] Haraldur Sigurdsson (*Melting the Earth: The History of Ideas on Volcanic Eruptions* [New York, 1999], 13) reminds us of the novelty of the Scottish physician James Hutton's declaration made

in 1788: "A volcano is not made on purpose to frighten superstitious people into fits of piety nor to overwhelm cities with destruction."

7 In 1789 Father Pietro d'Onofri wrote that when the gate of Pompeii was uncovered in 1755 the sculpted image of a phallus was to be seen on it, indicating that the city had dedicated itself to "the most sordid impudence," for which crimes it deserved divine destruction by fire. See Pietro d'Onofri, *Elogio estemporaneo per la gloriosa memoria di Carlo III, monarcha delle Spagne e delle Indie* [Naples, 1789], XCV. The remark is cited by Michele Arditi, in *Il fascino e l'amuleto contra il fascino presso gli antichi* (Naples, 1825), 1–2, where d'Onofri's facts as well as his conclusions are contested.

8 Stefano Delle Chiaje, "Cenno notomico patologico sulle ossa umane scavate in Pompei," is cited and summarized in Giulio Minervini, "Ossa e scheletri diseppeliti in Pompei," *Bullettino archeologico napolitano*, n.s. 3, no. 51 (July 1854): 1–3.

9 In the Roman catacombs Christian remains have usually been reburied under the authority of the Vatican. In Naples certain ossuaries filled up in time of the plague may strike visitors as "presenting a very disgusting appearance," in the words of Thomas Gray, *The Vestal, or a Tale of Pompeii* (1830; Louisville, 1977), 213n. 38, though the effect is more bizarre than disrespectful. The search for Christians in Pompeii has been disappointing. Novelists from Gray onward and even Gaetano Leofreddi, in his commemorative inscription of 1849 (*Diario della venuta e del soggiorno in Napoli di sua beatitudine Pio IX. P. M.* 18 [October 1849], reprinted in Soprintendenza archeologica di Pompei, Biblioteca apostolica vaticana, *Pio IX a Pompei: Memorie e testimonianze di un viaggio* [Naples, 1987], appendix), allowed the possibility that Saint Peter had preceded Pius. Raffaele Garucci, however, leaves the matter unresolved in his article "Si è rinvenuto finora alcuna cosa di cristiana credenza in Pompei?" *Bullettino archeologico napolitano* n.s. 2, no. 1 (July 1853): 8. Excavations in the 1860s revealed a house that was quickly named the "hostel of the Christians" (VII, 9, 11–12) on the basis of a graffito (*Corpus inscriptionum latinarum* IV.679). The graffito disappeared and Fiorelli was openly skeptical (see *Descrizione di Pompei* [Naples, 1875], 278–80). Matteo Della Corte later championed the site as evidence for Christians in Pompeii (*Case ed abitanti di Pompei*, 3d ed. [Naples, 1965], 204–5, nos. 398–401, and literature cited).

10 This attitude is inferred more from the obligatory condemnation of the manners of the ancient Pompeians found in virtually every traveler's account than it is from evidence regarding the actual treatment of human remains—about which surprisingly little has been written. The popular (and official) hostility shown toward Protestant burials in Rome in the eighteenth and nineteenth centuries gives some possible parallels. See Johan Beck-Friis, *The Protestant Cemetery in Rome* (1956; Malmö, 1988).

11 Johann Joachim Winckelmann, *Herkulanische Schriften Winckelmanns*, vol. 1, *Sendschreiben von den herculanischen Entdeckungen* (Mainz, 1997), 1:75.

12 Ibid.

13 Hylton A. Thomas, "Piranesi and Pompeii," *Kunstmuseets årsskrift* 39–42 (1952–55): 13–28, esp. 24, fig. 15.

14 The appearance of archaeological contexts, such as the Barracks of the Gladiators, helped Pompeii emerge from the shadow of Herculaneum as a center of learned and popular attention and to be established as the new paradigm in Vesuvian archaeology.

15 Egon Cesar Conte Corti, *The Destruction and Resurrection of Pompeii and Herculaneum*, trans. K. and R. Gregor Smith (London, 1951), 147–48. As sources Corti uses the *Giornale* and a letter from Emperor Joseph II to Empress Maria Theresa, Florence, April 21, 1769, in the Vienna State Archives (147n. 1). See also Fiorelli 1860 (note 4), 1:1.230 (April 7, 1768): "Dopo i Sovrani passarono ad osservare alcune stanze sottoposte, dove ancora si conserva uno scheletro intatto." Lawrence Richardson (*Pompeii: An Architectural History* [Baltimore, 1988], 234–40) carefully describes the house, including the bakery-bath suite on the lowest level.

16 Pierre Jacques Onésme Bergeret de Grancourt, *Voyage d'Italie, 1773–1774, avec les dessins de Fragonard*, ed. Jacques Wilhelm (Paris, 1948), 110–11, as cited in *The Golden Age of Naples: Art and Civilization under the Bourbons, 1734–1805* (Detroit, 1981), 2:279–80.

17 For the drawing, see *Pompei: Pitture e mosaici*, vol. 10, *La documentazione nell'opera di disegnatori e pittori dei secoli XVIII e XIX*, ed. Giovanni Pugliese Carratelli (Rome, 1995), 1, 5–6, 9 (fig. 9). The engraving after Fragonard's drawing, by Claude Fessard, is reproduced by Raleigh Trevelyan (*The Shadow of Vesuvius: Pompeii AD 79* [London, 1976], 48, fig. 29). Another drawing, by Pietro Fabris, dated 1774, is in the collection of the Society of Antiquaries, London. See Jan Jenkins and Kim Sloan, *Vases and Volcanoes: Sir William Hamilton and His Collection* (London, 1996), 43, fig. 16.

18 "One clearly sees that these … were overcome in the part of the house that was the most secure, but that they were powerless against the rain of ashes, which fell after that of the pumice, and one sees clearly that it was accompanied by water which fed into every part where the first rain of pumice had not" (Fiorelli 1860 [note 4], 1:268; my translation). Victims are for the first time referred to as "unfortunates" (*infelici*).

19 "Per dare una qualche testimonianza di quello che si asserisce avere osservato" (ibid.). La Vega described his excavation with unusual care, thus demonstrating an awareness of the importance of the archaeological context and the historic nature of this discovery. See ibid., 1:268–70 (December 12, 1772).

20 F. P. Latapie, "Description des fouilles de Pompéii (a. 1776)," *Rendiconti dell'Accademia di archeologia di Napoli* 28 (1953): 223–48, esp. 240.

21 Charles-Marguerite-Jean-Baptiste Mercier Dupaty, *Travels through Italy, in a Series of Letters; Written in the Year 1785, by President Dupaty* (London, 1788), 320.

22 Charles Dickens, *Pictures from Italy* (London, 1846), 159.

23 Ibid.

24 Dickens's understanding of the process of the eruption was probably prompted by that of the English antiquary Sir William Gell, who wrote: "Pompeii was not destroyed by an inundation of lava; its elevated position sheltered it from that fate: it was buried under that shower of stones and cinders of which Pliny speaks. Much of this matter appears to have been deposited in a liquid state; which is easily explained, for the vast volumes of steam sent up by the volcano descended in torrents of rain, which united with the ashes suspended in the air, or washed them, after they had fallen, into places where they could not well have penetrated in a dry state. Among other proofs of this, the skeleton of a woman was found in a cellar, enclosed within a mould of volcanic paste, which received and has retained a perfect impression of her form." Gell continued: "In the great eruption of 1779, minutely described by Sir William Hamilton, Ottaiano, a small town situated at the foot of Somma, most narrowly escaped similar destruction. The phenomena then observed may be presumed to correspond closely with that which occurred at Pompeii" (William Gell, *Pompeii: Its Destruction and Re-discovery* [New York, n.d. (after 1832)], 17).

25 Dupaty 1788 (note 21), 383. See also Chantal Grell, *Herculanum et Pompéi dans les récits des voyageurs français du XVIIIᵉ siècle* (Naples, 1982), 119.

26 Carlo Bonucci, *Pompei* (Naples, 1828), translated in Gray 1977 (note 9), 183.

27 Ibid., 181–82. See also T. L. Donaldson, *Pompeii, Illustrated with Picturesque Views* (London, 1827), 2:23.

28 Gray 1977 (note 9), 187.

29 Some fleeing victims may, in fact, have left their places of shelter before dawn—visible or no—on August 25, thus requiring lanterns in any event.

30 Ferdinand Gregorovius, *Euphorion: Eine Dichtung aus Pompeji* (Leipzig, 1858).

[31] Idem, *The Roman Journals of Ferdinand Gregorovius, 1852–1874*, ed. Friedrich Althaus and trans. Mrs. Gustavus W. Hamilton (London, 1911), 212 (Naples, August 15, 1864). Gregorovius was presumably referring to the younger of the two women who were cast together, though his interpretation of her fate contrasts noticeably with that of Layard and other observers.

[32] See Ferdinand Gregorovius, *Euphorion: Eine Dichtung aus Pompeji*, trans. Theodore Grosse, 2d ed. (Leipzig, 1884), 100.

[33] Poe wrote in his "Philosophy of Composition," first published in 1846, that "the death, then, of a beautiful woman is, unquestionably, the most poetical topic in the world." The classic study of this theme is Mario Praz, *The Romantic Agony*, trans. Angus Davidson, 2d ed. (London, 1951), esp. chap. 3, "The Shadow of the 'Divine Marquis,'" 93–186. For the eroticism of misfortune, see also Fritz Laupichler, "Misfortune," in *Encyclopedia of Comparative Iconography*, ed. Helene E. Roberts (Chicago, 1998), 2:609–13.

[34] Gautier's novel *Arria Marcella* has been discussed in Wolfgang Leppmann's *Pompeii in Fact and Fiction* (London, 1968), 136–40. Ironically, Gautier's character was seen as an example of modesty by earlier writers on Pompeii, like Donaldson 1827 (note 27) and Gray 1977 (note 9).

[35] Fiorelli 1860 (note 4), 2:248 (January–June 1831) and 3:114–15 (March 3–7, 1831); Robert Etienne, "Die letzten Stunden der Stadt Pompeji," in *Pompeji: Leben und Kunst in den Vesuvstädten*, 2d ed. (Recklinghausen, 1973), 53–58, esp. 56. The enthusiasm of certain male connoisseurs for a woman's foot may be found, for example, in pages of George Du Maurier's novel of artistic life, *Trilby* (New York, 1894); and Wilhelm Jensen's novel of Pompeii, *Gradiva: Ein pompejanisches Phantasiestück* (Dresden, 1903).

[36] Although Fiorelli was given full credit for the innovative discovery at the time and has ever since been recognized as the inventor of the process, descriptions of the actual casting technique have always been vague, lending support to the argument that credit should have been more widely given. Adolfo Venturi was the most prominent scholar to challenge Fiorelli's sole claim to the discovery. See Adolfo Venturi, *Memorie* (Milan, 1911), 101.

[37] Fiorelli proposed a standard admission fee in 1861, and the sum of two lire was instituted toward the end of the following year. The intent of the fee was to abolish tips and to raise money for additional custodians. In January 1863, after a month's receipts, Fiorelli reported that the excavations were running at a handsome profit. It was just as these preliminary results were being tabulated that the first of the casts was made (February 3, 1863). The publicity that followed the discovery helped draw more visitors to the excavations. On the admission fee, see *Pompeii: More Letters and Documents*, ed. Paola Poli Capri, 12 vols. (Rome, 1998), 1:26–32, 89–90, 97–103.

[38] Some visitors, like Edward Hutton, objected to the exhibition: "And if you have the courage to creep into that new museum by the gate you may see the images of those who suffered.... There they lie, the young matron beside the slave, the mother by the daughter, close together. ...Ah, why should our curiosity demand so horrible an outrage as this?" (Edward Hutton, *Naples and Campania Revisited* [London, 1958], 192–93). The museum opened in 1875 and was still "new" when Hutton wrote the essay on Pompeii, circa 1910. Compare also Augustus J. C. Hare, *Cities of Southern Italy and Sicily* (Philadelphia, [1882]), 218. Fiorelli's ministerial colleague Luigi Settembrini published an open letter to Fiorelli, in the first public response, that was both laudatory and critical. Settembrini evidently resented the celebrity then being accorded to Fiorelli, but this aspect of the event must be examined in another place. See Felice Barnabei, *Le "Memorie di un archeologo"* (Rome, 1991), 405–6, 415n. 3; and Giuseppe Fiorelli, *Appunti autobiografici*, ed. Stefano De Caro (Sorrento, 1994).

[39] Angelini, a prominent Neapolitan sculptor of the day, expressed his request and his intentions for the work in a letter from Naples to the Ministry of Public Instruction dated January 16, 1865. The letter, contained in the archive of the ministry, now in the Archivio centrale dello Stato in Rome, has been transcribed in *Giornale degli scavi di Pompei*, ed. Halsted B. Vander Poel and Paola Poli Capri (Rome, 1994), 7:X–XIV.

40 See Heinrich Brunn, "Scavi di Pompei, Cuma e Pesto," *Bullettino dell'Instituto di corrispondenza archeologica* (May–June 1863): 86–105, esp. 88–90. Fiorelli was the closest student of the casts, as attested by Brunn in the *Bullettino*. After his description of the four victims, Brunn deferred to Fiorelli, "who has not only examined these bodies more closely than anyone, but has also collected the observations made in his presence by archaeologists and antiquaries, artists, anatomists, and others." Brunn clearly expected that Fiorelli would eventually produce a definitive publication of the remains. It remains somewhat of a mystery that he did not produce such a study.

41 Hippolyte Taine, *Travels in Italy* (1865), cited by Robert Etienne, *Pompeii: The Day a City Died*, trans. Caroline Palmer (New York, 1992), 159.

42 See Anne Hollander, *Seeing through Clothes* (Harmondsworth, 1975), esp. 274–87.

43 For the modesty in women's dress favored by the court of the saintly Maria Christina, see Harold Acton, *The Last Bourbons of Naples* (London, 1961), 75–76. In addition to the young queen's influence, Ferdinand II was, for most of his reign (1830–59), under the influence of his confessor, Monsignor Celestino Cocle.

44 For the history of this collection, see *Il gabinetto segreto del Museo archeologico di Napoli*, ed. Stefano De Caro (Naples, 2000), esp. 9–22.

45 Società napoletana di storia patria, manuscript XXIX.C.I. See Mario Pagano, "Una legge ritrovata: Il progetto di legge per il riordinamento del R. museo di Napoli e degli scavi di antichità del 1848 e il ruolo di G. Fiorelli," *Archivio storico per le provincie napoletane* 112 (1994): 351–414.

46 Pagano 1994 (note 45), 393 (art. 72).

47 Ibid., 412 (art. 289, item 13); see also 370.

48 Ibid., 370n. 41 (Archivio di Stato di Napoli, Ministero della pubblica istruzione, fs. 317/9): "ma la proposta fu respinta dal Re il 14 novembre 1848." The plan was eventually implemented.

49 Giuseppe Fiorelli, *Museo nazionale di Napoli: Raccolta pornografica* (Naples, 1866), preface. Concerning Fiorelli's charge of "religious hypocrisy," a contemporary anecdote illustrates the extent to which religion and government worked together in the last days of the Bourbons of Naples. "When Victor Emmanuel first entered Naples to take possession of his new kingdom, he received, amidst many congratulations and submissions, one of strange character. An ecclesiastical dignitary approached towards his Majesty, and inquired in a low voice, but with an air of the utmost candour and simplicity, to whom he was to make his *report of the confessions*." One is meant to conclude that the secrets of the confessional had been regularly transmitted to the Bourbon police under the previous regime. See *Blackwood's Magazine* 101 (April 1867): 420.

50 See *Pio IX a Pompei: Memorie e testimonianze di un viaggio: Catalogo della mostra; Pompei scavi, Casina dell'Aquila, luglio–settembre 1987* (Naples, [1987]), 71–72.

51 Ibid., 72. The papal visit and the respect shown toward the excavations, as well as the gracious acceptance of a selection of artifacts, may well have been intended to answer the challenge to papal infallibility shown several years earlier (in 1845) by the Seventh Congress of Italian Scientists, whose session at Pompeii had been presided over by the youthful Fiorelli himself.

52 The new freedom did not immediately result in universal sympathy with the ancient way of life, as an 1861 observation made by Pedro de Alarcón indicates. The Spanish man of letters found in the pornographic collection "the Providential explanation of the destruction of Pompeii," a sentiment with which Thomas Gray thirty years earlier would have concurred. Alarcón is cited in De Caro 2000 (note 44), 19. Thomas Gray wrote: "the indecent paintings in the bed-rooms of the young girls, the charm *contra sterilitatem* which there seems little reason to doubt were worn by the ladies about the neck, as in modern times a cross or an eye-glass; the symbol over the oven [i.e., the phallus], etc., all serve to show how deep was the moral degradation from which Christianity rescued mankind" (Gray 1977 [note 9]), 203n. 20).

53 Raffaele Gargiulo, *Cenni storici e descrittivi dell'edificio del Museo nazionale* (Naples, 1864), 40.

54 Charles Ernest Beulé, *Drame du Vesuve* (Paris, 1872), 1–2.

55 Modern forensic pathologists would interpret this gesture as a "pugilistic stance," character-istic of victims whose bodies had been burned or exposed to high temperatures at the time of death.

56 See *Giornale degli scavi di Pompei*, n.s. 3 (1875): 173: [23 April 1875] 23 (Reg. VI, Is. 14). The cast has been illustrated in many books on Pompeii. See, for example, Pierre Gusman, *Pompei* (London, 1900), 17. (In his text Gusman confuses this woman with the "pregnant woman" of 1863.) Amedeo Maiuri illustrated the woman of 1875 ("una giovane e bella vittima dell'eruzione") in the many editions of his guide to Pompeii in the popular Ministry of Public Instruction series.

57 "Body of a Woman (Cadavere di donna)," in Yusef Komunyakaa, *Talking Dirty to the Gods: Poems* (New York, 2000), 42. I am indebted to Angela Salas for this reference.

58 Amedeo Cicchitti, who in the 1980s refined the casting process to obtain "the first transparent cast," was at that time unable to locate Fiorelli's first cast of the pregnant woman. See Amedeo Cicchitti, *Pompei: Il primo calco trasparente (Diario di uno scavo)* (L'Aquila, [1993]), 24.

59 For example, Joannes Overbeck, *Pompeji in seinen Gebäuden, Alterthümern und Kunstwerken für Kunst- und Alterthumsfreunde dargestellt* (Leipzig, 1856); August Mau, *Pompeii: Its Life and Art*, trans. Francis W. Kelsey (London, 1899); idem, *Pompeji in Leben und Kunst* (Leipzig, 1900). Both authors enjoyed great popularity in the heyday of historiography that was foreseen by Beulé.

60 Luigi Settembrini was the author of the revolutionary pamphlet *Protesta del popolo delle Due Sicilie*, published anonymously in 1847. He was imprisoned for revolutionary activities but con-tinued to use his pen effectively until the fall of the Bourbons in 1860. Subsequently he became inspector general of public instruction and held the chair of Italian literature in the Univer-sity of Naples. The excerpt from Settembrini's contemporary open letter to Fiorelli is cited in Emilio Magaldi, *Pompei e il suo dolore* (Naples, 1930), 103–4, 105n. 78.

61 It may be inferring too much from the quoted passage to say that Settembrini favored the burial (reburial?) of the victims, yet his youthful habit of reciting from Ugo Foscolo's poem "I sepol-cri" of 1806 reflects a lifelong respect for the honored dead. See Luigi Settembrini, *Ricordanze della mia vita* (Milan, 1964), 1:38. The church has frequently opposed the cult of the dead in Italian nationalism, as the history of the Roman Pantheon illustrates.

Nero, and yet there are far more Fourth-Style paintings than any other style despite the fact that the bulk of them were painted in a space of 17 years. Most buildings in the town suffered some damage in the earthquake and the repairs are evident enough. Some houses were abandoned, and only in the amphitheatre and the Temple of Isis were repairs finished by AD 79. An inscription records that a freedman rebuilt the latter in the name of his son, Numerius Popidius Celsinus, a boy six years old, as a means of securing him a seat on the town council. This perhaps reflects the changed social complexion of Pompeii in these years, when many of the older patricians had left the town and newly enriched freedmen began to win political power. It may seem curious that such a temple should have been totally rebuilt at a time when those of the official cults were still in ruins. The explanation may lie in the fact that the cult of Isis was a popular one among the very slaves who now had so much influence.

In the last years of the city many old patrician houses were bought up and subdivided, or turned into lodging houses or commercial premises. Any available room with a street frontage was turned into a small shop. Sometimes a whole house, as for example the Villa of the Mysteries, was turned over to industrial production. In other cases a few rooms of a house were made into a bakery or a fullery. The whole aspect of Pompeian streets was changing as upper storey rooms were added, and balconies and upstairs windows penetrated street façades. One might justly claim that if the eruption of Vesuvius had not occurred in AD 79 the old Pompeii, familiar to us by its fine houses and splendid paintings, might have largely disappeared within the next half century.

Ostia is another well-preserved Roman city, but it was not destroyed by a violent natural catastrophe like Pompeii. It was gradually abandoned until its buildings collapsed one by one. Precious marbles, statues and columns were torn from the decaying buildings to turn up as far away as Pisa and Salerno. For over a millennium the site was one of almost complete desolation and abandonment, until it slowly began to be uncovered in the mid-nineteenth century. The pace of excavation increased in the period 1938–42, when most of the city known today was uncovered.

As Ostia was abandoned gradually there are fewer spectacular finds than at Pompeii, where entire painted rooms, wooden shutters and furniture, and even foodstuffs, regularly turn up. Yet in many ways Ostia is a more typical Roman town than Pompeii, which had deep Oscan roots, and whose people never fully accepted Roman ways. Ostia was the harbour town of Rome, and was thus particularly well-placed to reflect the styles and tastes of the capital. Whereas Pompeii died in AD 79, at a time when architectural and artistic styles were in a process of rapid change, Ostia lived on. The

118

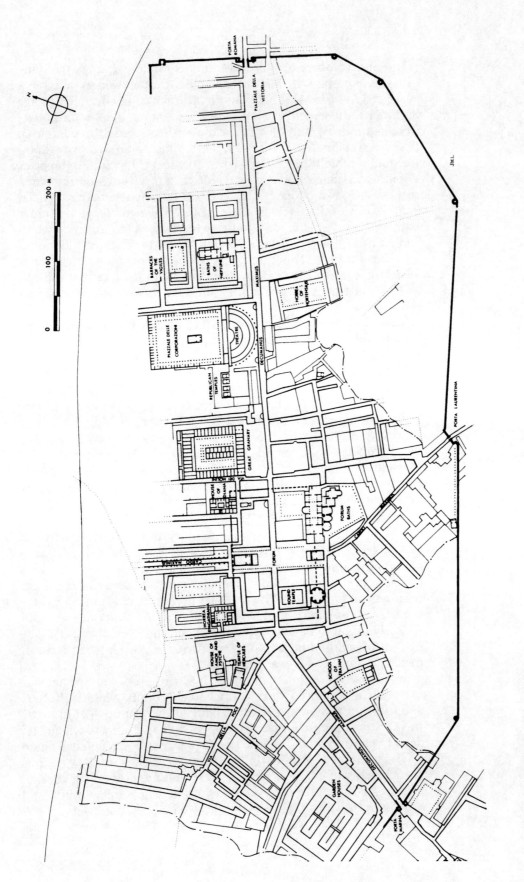

67 Ostia, general plan

20

town was practically rebuilt in the second century AD using all the techniques of brick-faced concrete which had been evolved in the course of the first century AD. The typical buildings of Ostia are not sumptuous houses and villas, but tall apartment blocks, baths and warehouses. While Pompeii survives as a leisured country town with elegant, sprawling houses, Ostia was an Imperial port, jammed with the functional housing blocks which must have been a feature of Rome itself. Ostia is therefore a fundamental document of the urban and social changes which took place in the later Empire, and in addition illustrates the whole life of a Roman city from the fourth century BC to the fifth century AD.

Ostia is situated on the south bank of the Tiber close to its mouth, at a distance of about 25 kilometres from Rome. The road that links it with Rome, the Via Ostiensis, leaves the capital through the Porta Trigemina and runs close to the south bank of the river for some 15 kilometres, at which point it meets high ground. This high ground was also the source of Ostia's water supply, as can be seen from the remains of brick piers belonging to an aqueduct of Imperial date. From the high ground the road descends into a marshy plain. This section of the road was laid upon wooden piles driven into the soft subsoil.

Ostia was founded as a defensive fortress to protect Rome's coastline. Marauding bands of Gauls were still active in the area after the great invasion of 390 BC, and in 349 BC Greek fleets had ravaged the coast from Antium to the Tiber estuary. Colonies composed of Roman citizens were established, at Antium in 338, Anxur in 329, and Minturnae in 296 BC. In 311 BC ships were built to patrol the coast, and *quaestores Italici* were placed in charge of naval defences (267 BC). Ostia was part of the series of coastal forts. Although the exact date of its foundation is not known, it can probably be placed between 349 and 338 BC.

The outline of the original *castrum* can still be seen, although the actual walls have largely disappeared (fig. 67). It was rectangular and covered an area of about 2.2 hectares (5½ acres). The usual two streets, the *decumanus* running east/west, and the *cardo* running north/south, divided the fort into four areas and intersected in the middle, the area where the later Forum was built. Traces of the four gates belonging to the fort have been found under later buildings of the town. The eastern branch of the decumanus led directly to Rome, but the roads to the south and west were somewhat more irregular. As at Pompeii, the line of these roads is preserved in the layout of the later, developed town. It has, however, been suggested that the southern branch of the cardo, which leads away from the castrum in a south-easterly direction, was in fact originally a part of the same road as the Via della Foce which leads out of the Porta Marina or west gate of the castrum in a north-westerly direction. Thus the original Via Laurentina led directly to the mouth of the

120

21

river, and had to be diverted when the castrum was built. That the original road from Rome followed the line of the eastern decumanus is less likely because the latter is dictated by the siting of the castrum.

At about the time of Sulla (around 80 BC) new walls were built around Ostia enclosing an area of 63.5 hectares (160 acres), or almost 30 times the extent of the original castrum (fig. 67). Such a massive increase in the city limits must mean one of two things: either the city had already expanded beyond the lines of the old castrum by that date; or a great increase in populaton was envisaged. Unfortunately any attempt to gauge the size of pre-Sullan Ostia is hampered by the fact that not all the area around the castrum has yet been excavated, and because much of the area was totally rebuilt in the second century AD. There is very little archaeological evidence of buildings made of permanent materials before the end of the second century BC. However, some painted terracottas were found in the pre-Sullan layers, and these suggest mud-brick buildings with timber roofs. Timber was plentiful in the district and may have been a common building material in the early period of Ostia's growth. So the pre-Sullan town may have been larger than it at first appears. Also, a glance at the area south of the theatre and to the east of the Via dei Molini shows a haphazard street plan which may well date back to an earlier period of uncontrolled building activity. Certainly, towards the end of the second century BC a number of prosperous peristyle and atrium houses were built, and it is also to this period that we must attribute Ostia's first stone temple, the Temple of Hercules. It is perhaps no coincidence that the first signs of prosperity in Ostia came at the time of the Gracchi when the importation of cheap corn and the wars against the Cimbri and Teutones brought prosperity to the harbour town.

The Sullan wall circuit is trapezoidal in shape, and its line is partly dictated by the coastline and the river. The three main gates are the Porta Marina through which the western decumanus runs to the sea-shore, the Porta Laurentina through which the southern cardo runs on its way south, and the Porta Romana which marks the end of the eastern decumanus and the beginning of the Via Ostiensis. During the last century of the Republic, atrium and peristyle houses continued to be built, and porticoes on tufa piers began to appear along some of the main streets. Perhaps the most important development of the period was the rebuilding of the north-east corner of the town. The land adjacent to the river was declared public property by the Roman praetor, and the whole area re-planned on orderly lines. The regular planning of the area north of the eastern decumanus contrasts starkly with the haphazard development south of it, where private building had run amok during the Republic. Even the four late Republican temples just west of where the theatre was later built are planned in a neat and orderly

121

68 Ostia, plan of the Claudian and Trajanic harbours

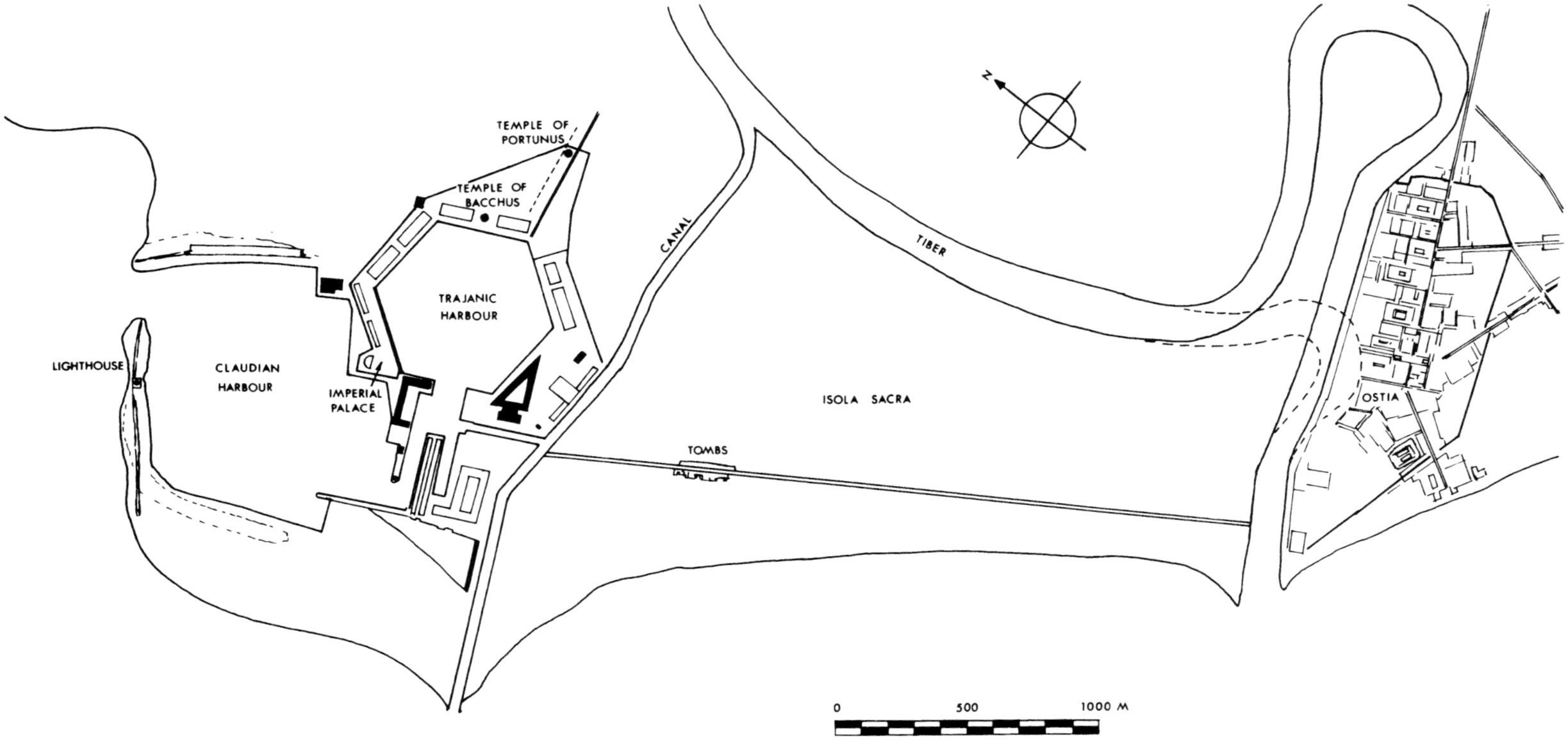

LIGHTHOUSE

CLAUDIAN HARBOUR

IMPERIAL PALACE

TRAJANIC HARBOUR

TEMPLE OF BACCHUS

TEMPLE OF PORTUNUS

CANAL

TOMBS

ISOLA SACRA

TIBER

N

OSTIA

0   500   1000 M

fashion. At some time during the late Republic or the early Augustan period the centre of the old castrum where the cardo and decumanus meet was cleared of buildings and laid out as the Forum. At the south end a temple of Rome and Augustus was built. It is hexastyle and is raised on a high podium. Like the Temple of Divine Julius in the Roman Forum it had a rostra in front of the porch, and access to the podium was by two lateral staircases. Like buildings in Rome it was sheathed in Carrara marble, and the sculptures were done by artists brought from the capital.

The river harbour at Ostia had become increasingly inadequate during the later Republic because of the bigger merchant ships used, the growing volume of shipping and the narrowness of the river (it was only 100 metres wide where it flowed past Ostia). The mouth of the river, too, was beginning to silt up and the resultant sand-bar was a hazard to shipping. Julius Caesar planned a harbour at Ostia, but the project was dropped, and it was not until the time of Claudius that the idea was revived. The reaction of the Emperor's architects was that the scheme would be prohibitively expensive, and they tried to dissuade him (Dio Cassius, 60. 11. 3). However, the Emperor persisted and excavation work for the harbour began in AD 42 at a spot four kilometres north of the harbour mouth (fig. 68). A huge shallow basin about 1,100 metres wide was cut out of the coastline and extended into the sea by two curving moles. Also, a canal was built to link the harbour directly with a bend in the Tiber. This canal had the important secondary effect of providing an extra outlet for the river and helping protect Rome from flooding. The two moles were built of enormous travertine blocks each weighing six or seven tonnes, tied together by iron clamps. In the middle of the left mole was built a lighthouse which rested upon the ship which Caligula had built to bring the great obelisk from Heliopolis for his circus (see p. 92). Pliny (*Natural History*, 16. 202) describes this ship as having carried a ballast of 800 tonnes of lentils and as having a main mast that could be spanned only by four men linking arms. A ship of such dimensions using ancient construction methods seemed an impossibility until recent excavations revealed parts of the ship and the famous lighthouse (fig. 69). The ship was 104 metres long, 20.30 metres wide and had six decks. Its displacement was 7,400 tonnes and it must have been manned by a crew of 700 or 800 men. The hulk was filled with concrete and sunk to provide the foundations for the lighthouse. Sadly, the Claudian harbour was not a success. Tacitus (*Annals*, 15. 18. 3) records that in AD 62 200 vessels in the harbour were destroyed by a storm. Other ancient sources make it clear that the Alexandrian corn fleet still continued to dock at Puteoli even when the Claudian harbour was complete, no doubt to avoid the hazardous sea passage to Ostia and the dangers that lurked even in the harbour itself. Indeed Nero planned a canal from Lake Avernus (near Puteoli) to Ostia, with the intention

123

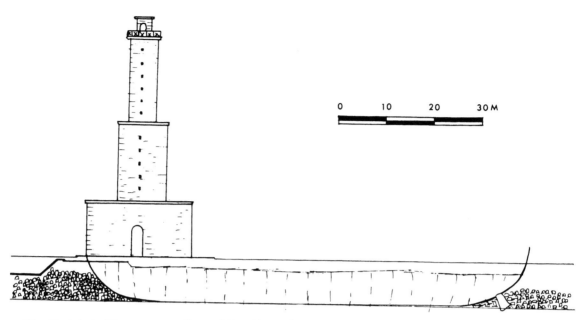

69 Sketch to illustrate the lighthouse at Ostia resting upon the hull of Caligula's galley (after O. Testaguzza)

of providing Rome's corn supply with a sheltered route which would avoid the stormy west coast, and the harbour at Ostia. The problems of providing a safe harbour for Rome and securing Rome's corn supply were not resolved until the time of Trajan.

Trajan excavated an enormous hexagonal basin inland of the old harbour to the south-east (fig. 68). The two harbours were linked by a canal which was essentially a rebuilding of the old Claudian canal. A second canal, again based on an earlier one, ran to the south of the harbour and linked a bend of the Tiber with the sea and the harbour. The basin itself was of huge dimensions with a maximum diameter of 700 metres. It was surrounded by large concrete *horrea* or warehouses. In type they differ from earlier Ostian warehouses in that the rooms are not grouped around a central courtyard. Instead they have two rows of rooms back-to-back, probably to save space. One of these warehouses on the south-east side of the basin had a raised floor which suggests that it was used for storing grain, and a ramp led up to the floor above. Into the embankment walls of the harbour was set a row of travertine mooring posts and there were probably facilities for over 100 ships. Along the quay were found numbered columns which probably correspond to the mooring berths. In this way gangs of men could easily be allotted to particular ships. Other monuments around the harbour basin include a building complex in which much fine statuary was found. The complex, which lies on the west side of the harbour at a point where it commands views of both Trajan's and Claudius' harbour, is often called the 'Imperial Palace'. Its position, fine reticulate construction and amenities, including a bath building, may well prove the attribution to be a correct one, although Lugli has argued that it is in

124

fact the Forum of the town of Portus. In the centre of the north-east side is a circular temple of Bacchus who appears in the well-known Torlonia harbour relief. Nearby were found fragments of a colossal statue of Trajan in military dress. As it was so far from Ostia a small settlement grew up around the harbour and seems to have been concentrated to the south and east of the basin. The eastern area was enclosed in a tight triangular wall in the time of Constantine. At its apex was a third-century circular temple, commonly known as the Temple of Portunus. The main gate through which the Via Portuense ran lay close to the temple. Beside the road ran an aqueduct, large portions of which have recently been discovered.

The construction of these harbour facilities led to a wave of new buildings at Ostia which began in Trajan's reign and was largely completed by the time of Antoninus Pius. The volume of goods which now passed through Ostia was the reason for its prosperity, which is reflected in the more or less total rebuilding of the old town. The architectural revolution in Rome (see p. 102) had occurred at the time of Nero, but its effects only reached Ostia during the reign of Domitian, just in time for the influx of new wealth.

The western parts of Ostia were radically transformed under Trajan. The whole area between the Via della Foce and the river was rebuilt, as well as the buildings in the extreme west of the town by the river mouth. The eastern part of the town would have presented a great contrast to the brick-faced Trajanic work. The eastern decumanus was still lined with the tufa temples and houses of the Republic along with some reticulate walls of the early empire.

In the reign of Hadrian even more radical transformations took place, and half of the surviving remains of Ostia date from this period. Two areas were completely replanned: the area between the Forum and the river, and the area north of the eastern decumanus and east of the theatre. Both areas were public property and required not only clear, logical planning but also dignity. A large Capitolium was laid out at the northern end of the Forum (fig. 70). Brick-built and sheathed in marble, it was raised on a high podium, presumably so that it could dominate the tall surrounding blocks. Interestingly, the total height of the building to the apex of the gable is 70 Roman feet (21 metres), which suggests that the surrounding buildings were built to the full 60 Roman feet allowed in the Trajanic building regulations (*Epit. de Caes.*, 13).

A radical replanning of the northern cardo provided a monumental approach to the Forum from the river. The point where the cardo met the river was a landing place of importance where the Emperor or any visiting dignitary would land. The road from the river to the Capitolium was laid out on broad, straight lines and was flanked by brick porticoes. The whole adjacent area was also rebuilt at that time.

The large-scale rebuilding under Hadrian was greatly facilitated

125

70 Ostia, the Capitolium, *c*. AD 120–130

71 Ostia, Forum Baths: the frigidarium, *c*. AD 160

by the expansion of the brick industry (see p. 77), and by the end of Hadrian's reign reticulate work had entirely disappeared. Late in his reign another section of the town, the area east of the theatre, was rebuilt. New buildings included the Baths of Neptune and the barracks of the *vigiles*, along with a brick portico to flank the adjacent stretch of the eastern decumanus. By the middle of the second century AD the city was almost fully built up. There were few open spaces except the public gardens behind the theatre. Even the four temples west of the theatre were surrounded by buildings.

Demolition and rebuilding went on in Antonine times, but the pace had begun to slacken. Perhaps the most interesting buildings of the period are the baths. At Pompeii there were only two public baths until the final years of the city, when the Central Baths were begun. In Ostia 18 public baths have been excavated, a reflection on the changing bathing habits of Romans during the Empire. Some of them are large and imposing structures, for example the Forum Baths (fig. 75), built at the time of Antoninus Pius. The frigidarium (fig. 71) is conservative in its layout, with eight columns supporting a vaulted roof and cold plunges to north and south. However, the series of warm and hot rooms which project boldly out from the lines of the old castrum are more interesting. The most westerly is octagonal and presents four big windows to the afternoon sun, which, in the absence of heating pipes in the walls, suggests that it was a *heliocaminus* or sun room of the type found at Hadrian's villa. The oval room next to it has a bench against the walls, underfloor heating and heated walls: therefore it was probably a sweating room. Next are two warm rooms with big windows, and at the end a large caldarium or hot room. The irregular triangle to the south of the baths was left open as a palaestra. It was presumably one more welcome open space in an increasingly crowded city centre.

Other interesting buildings of the Antonine period are the School of Trajan, with its apsidal hall and long nymphaeum running the whole length of the garden. Also built at this time were the House of Diana and the Horrea Epagathiana, with its remarkable dressed-brick doorway (fig. 74). As the second century progressed the tempo of building slowed even further. A little building went on in the area between the eastern decumanus and the river. The great Granary was rebuilt under Commodus, and the Augustan theatre was rebuilt in brick and re-opened at the beginning of the reign of Septimius Severus.

At this point we should pause and look at the housing blocks and warehouses which are such a conspicious feature of second-century AD Ostia. Tall buildings had existed in Rome since the third century BC as we know from Livy's tale (21. 62. 3) about an ox finding its way up to a third storey of a house in the Forum Boarium. What was a necessity for the poor later became a fashion for the rich. By the end of the Roman Empire there were 25 insulae to every domus in

127

72 Ostia, insula,
second century AD

Rome. Insulae, or apartment blocks, also existed in Pompeii, and in its final years Pompeii was undergoing changes which might have transformed it into a city more like second-century Ostia instead of the leisured, sprawling town that has survived. However, Ostia lived on to meet the demands of the second century AD, when scarcity of space made tall buildings a necessity.

The Ostian insulae probably reflected Roman models. They were built of brick-faced concrete which was designed to be seen and not covered with stucco. The rather severe façades are often relieved by a doorway of decorative brick or a balcony (fig. 72). In the absence of cheap window glass, lighting was a problem which greatly occupied architects. Big windows faced the street and the inner courtyards which formed the centre of the blocks. The House of Diana is a convenient example of a typical insula (fig. 73). It will be seen from the ground plan that only the west and south sides of the building faced onto the street. The other two sides of the block abutted against other buildings and could draw no light from those sides. Therefore the architect has placed a courtyard to light the rooms on the north and east sides. On the street frontages there were shops on the ground floor and staircases led up to the apartments on the upper floors. In the centre of the courtyard was a water cistern which served all the residents. Lavatories were scarce in insulae, usually only one on each floor. The height of some of these blocks must have been considerable to judge by the Trajanic regulations banning buildings over 60 Roman feet. The number of storeys in such a block can be roughly calculated by the thickness of the walls at ground

73 Ostia, one block of the Garden Houses (above), and the Insula of Diana, later second century AD (below)

128

29

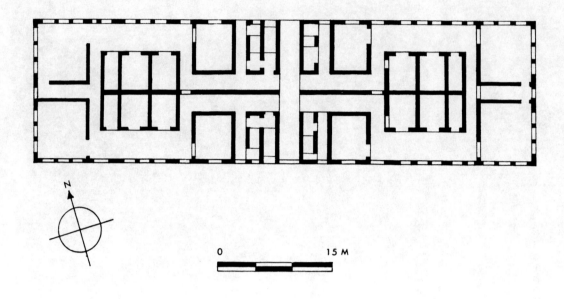

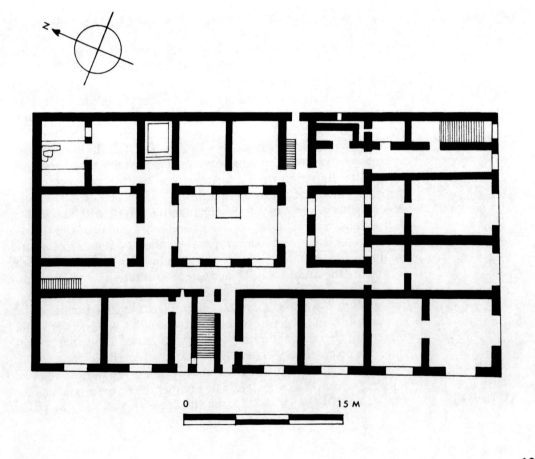

30

129

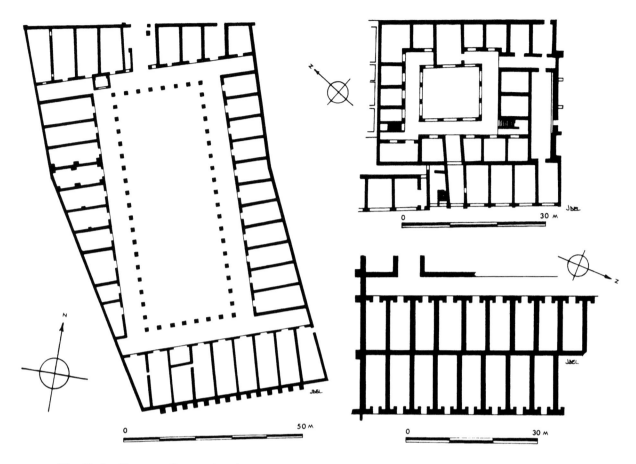

74 Ostia, Horrea of
Hortensius, granary
c. AD 30–40: plan (left);
Ostia, Horrea
Epagathiana, warehouse
c. AD 145–150: plan
(right, above); Ostia,
Antonine Horrea: plan
(right, below)

level. For example a wall 50 cm thick suggests two storeys, 80 cm
four storeys and 95 cm five storeys.

The so-called Garden Houses represent an interesting planned
development. Here two identical housing blocks are set in a large
garden. Each block (fig. 73) is divided by a corridor into two halves
and in each half are two entirely self-contained housing units back to
back. Six outside staircases lead to the upstairs apartments.

There is a large concentration of warehouses, mainly on the river
side of Ostia. Their capacity is clearly greater than the needs of Ostia
itself would warrant. Most of them were designed to store grain until
it was required in Rome. The grain warehouses usually have raised
floors for dryness, and conform to two types. One type has a number
of rooms on four sides of a colonnaded courtyard (fig. 74). The
second type, which eventually superseded the first, has rows of
rooms back to back and thus made more economical use of space.
Not all the warehouses were for grain; some were for the storage of
oil, wine and other commodities. Local traders and the repre-
sentatives of overseas shippers had offices in Ostia. Sixty-one such
offices were found in the Piazzale delle Corporazioni behind the
theatre. On the floor in front of each shop is a mosaic explaining the

130

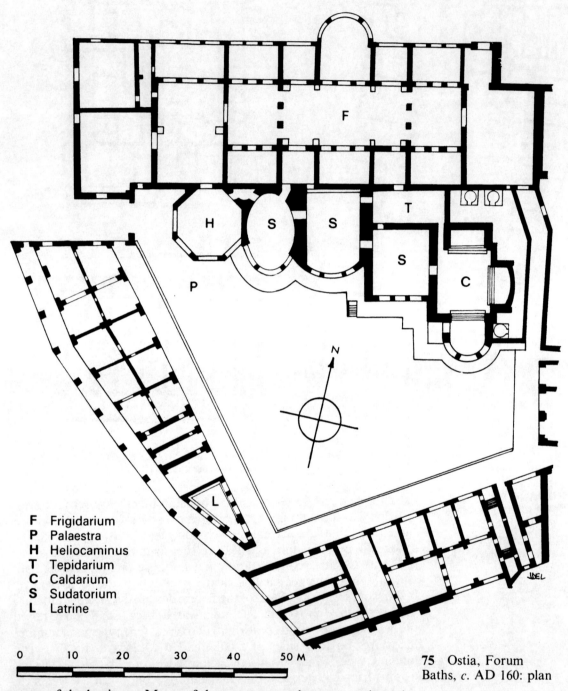

F Frigidarium
P Palaestra
H Heliocaminus
T Tepidarium
C Caldarium
S Sudatorium
L Latrine

0   10   20   30   40   50 M

75 Ostia, Forum
Baths, *c.* AD 160: plan

nature of the business. Many of them represent the corn trade and symbols associated with Africa are common. One mosaic bears the words '*stat(io) Sabratensium*' and an elephant, a reference to the town of Sabratha in Tripolitania.

As a seaport Ostia attracted a wide range of foreign traders and

131

businessmen. The cosmopolitan nature of Ostia is reflected in the wide range of religious buildings found there. As well as a large number of conventional temples there is evidence of a flourishing Imperial cult, as well as buildings devoted to the cults of Cybele and Isis. A large number of mithraea have been found, mainly dating to the later second and the third centuries. Even a synagogue has been found dating to the first century AD with evidence that it was still in use in the fourth century AD.

Most of the Severan era was devoted to the restoration of baths and granaries, but in the middle of this quiet period an exceptionally ambitious project was begun, the Round Temple. It is difficult to explain such a scheme at this late date (suggested dates are in the region of AD 222–244). At a time of declining wealth it would almost certainly have been the product of Imperial patronage, either by Alexander Severus or Gordian III whose father lived at Ostia. The temple, sited just west of the Forum, is essentially a smaller version of the Pantheon with its circular drum, pierced by alternately round and square exedras, supporting a dome. A large, rectangular, colonnaded courtyard was built in front of the temple and provided another much-needed open space in the congested central area.

As land prices dropped in the third century, more open spaces were created, such as the small square south of the eastern decumanus and east of the Forum. A second square, the Piazzale della Vittoria, was created just inside the Porta Romana.

Ostia remained a prosperous city up to the time of the Severans, but as Imperial trade ran down in the third century people began to move to the harbour, at first called Portus Ostiae, then Portus Romae and finally Portus, when it became an independent authority. Excavations in the area between the decumanus and the river give a dismal impression of impoverishment in the late Empire. However, in other parts of the town there is evidence that many large houses were kept up and several new ones built as land values dropped and senatorial families with big households moved in. Often walls of old insulae were re-used to save money, but the new houses were quite lavish in their interior decoration and use of space. The House of Amor and Psyche is a good example of a late Imperial Ostian domus (fig. 76). A vestibule containing two rows of benches for waiting visitors leads into a wide colonnaded passage running the length of the house. To the left are three rooms with floors and walls lined with polychrome marble. At the end of the corridor is an ample *oecus* with marble-lined walls and *opus sectile* floor. In an angle was a staircase which led to an upper storey which probably only extended over the four smaller rooms. Nearly half the ground area of the house is taken up by an open garden. Against the back wall is a row of five round-headed fountain niches lined with marble and glass mosaic.

In AD 314 Constantine stripped Ostia of her municipal rights and

132

transferred them to Portus, which henceforth became the seat of the bishopric. Even so Ostia retained a measure of prosperity throughout the fourth century. Opulent houses were still built and the baths kept in repair until the end of the century, when civic authority began to break down. By AD 414 the poet Rutilius wrote that the only glory remaining to Ostia was the glory of Aeneas who, legend says, landed there. By the sixth century only a few inhabitants lived in the ruins of buildings, half-demolished and stripped of their marble. The dead were buried in the baths and the theatre. The road from Rome to Ostia was overgrown and the Tiber a river without boats. No longer the port of Rome, little attempt was made to defend it from barbarian incursions. Finally, the area became malarial and was abandoned.

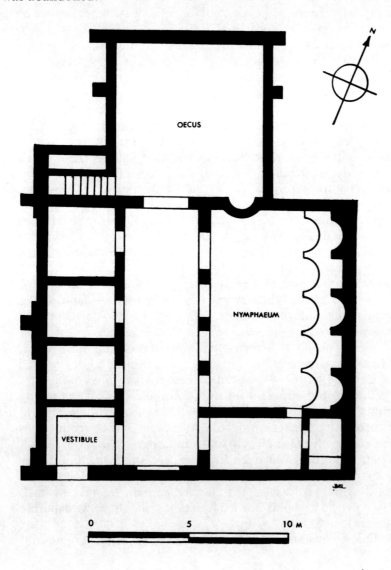

76 Ostia, House of Amor and Psyche *c.* AD 300: plan

133

PORTUS IN CONTEXT

Simon Keay and Martin Millett

The foregoing chapters have presented and drawn together the new evidence for the development of Portus. It now seems worthwhile to stand back from this detail and to reassess our general understanding of the site. In the first instance, we want to draw upon the new material to advance our understanding of the character and functions of Portus. In particular, we attempt to gauge the importance of the urban component of the port, analyse the significance of its planning, and interpret the whole complex as an ideological statement about Roman power. In this discussion, we have not attempted to be comprehensive, but rather wish to explore ideas on a broad canvass.[1]

PRE-CLAUDIAN PORTUS

Before the construction of the harbour complex was initiated by Claudius, it is well known that Rome relied for her seaborne commerce on the river port at Ostia and the harbours in the bay of Naples, particularly Puteoli (Camodeca 1994). Goods on ships arriving in the bay of Naples were transshipped to vessels that travelled on to Ostia, or otherwise were carried overland. Similarly, ships also stood at anchor off the mouth of the Tiber at Ostia so that cargoes could be transferred to barges in order to move upstream to either Ostia or Rome (Rickman 1980: 18, 46). These processes of transshipment were evidently inconvenient and this had led to consideration of constructing a new port at the mouth of the Tiber under Julius Caesar (**B5**; see above, p. 11).

Although we have no evidence for the development of any harbour facilities at Portus before the Claudian period there was certainly occupation in the area. The geomorphological evidence clearly indicates a stable coastal strip along which there presumably ran a road. To the south of the Tiber, this archaic coastal route was refashioned as the Via Severiana in the early third century (Lauro and Claridge 1998: 39). It is possible that it continued north from Ostia, although there is no firm evidence for its existence until the late first century AD (see below, p. 299). By contrast, the evidence for the existence of a route running alongside the Tiber from Rome is better known. Our survey provides evidence of an early first-century AD building (structure 19.3) adjacent to the bank of the Tiber, which probably should be understood in the context of the use of the river for shipping goods upstream by barge from Ostia to Rome. We also infer the existence of a road hidden beneath the modern flood protection bank beside the Tiber here (see above, pp. 279–81). To the northeast, recent excavations have uncovered traces of the pre-Claudian Via Campana to the west of modern Ponte Galeria, one of whose original functions would have been to carry salt inland from pans in the lagoons behind the coastal dunes. Indeed, geomorphological evidence confirms the lagoonal environment in this zone. If the Via Campana did intersect with a putative coastal route in the pre-Claudian period, the junction between the two could have acted as a focus for early settlement. To date, however, our only evidence for this period comes in the form of a farmstead on the landward side of the salt-marshes, as well as a light scatter of sherds across the survey area. Other farmsteads recently investigated nearby have been associated with the exploitation of the salt marshes (Morelli, Olcese and Zevi 2004). In general, the land to the north of the Tiber seems to have remained a backwater, subject to periodic inundations by the river.

THE CLAUDIAN HARBOUR

The construction of the Claudian harbour was an enormous project and one that took more than twenty years to complete. It is almost certainly the largest public project initiated by Claudius and debate seems to have been generated about the practicability of the plans (**B9** and **B10**). The scale

and length of time involved were considerable and mean that we should try to understand how it might have developed during the building process. Particular care should be taken not to read back from the completed second-century harbour to understand the early phases of the project, but instead to attempt to look at the developments in their contemporary context.

The land chosen for the new harbour was marginal to Ostia. It lay 3 km to the north of the Tiber mouth, at the point where the course of the river curves towards the south. If our reconstruction of the pattern of Claudian canals is correct, the harbour location would appear to have been determined by the most appropriate position for digging canals between the river and the sea in order to alleviate flooding upstream (see, however, pp. 36–7). Much has been written about the evidence for the Claudian canals, but two points deserve to be stressed. Firstly, the monumental inscription set up to commemorate their completion (A1; Fig. 9.1) was dedicated in AD 46, very soon after the building project had been initiated, and may have adorned the attic of a monumental arch (see above, p. 36). The early date of this great inscription implies that the canals were a primary objective of the work. Secondly, although it is often presumed that the canals were excavated 'to provide communications for his new harbour' (Meiggs 1973: 159), the inscription says only that they were dug for the purpose of his construction of the harbour and freed the city from

the threat of flooding. Since it provides no indication of the scale or indeed the number of canals commemorated, it may be a mistake to assume that the initial plans for the harbour envisaged the canals being the principal route for barges moving upstream (see below). Both canals were probably important for transport associated with the construction of the harbour, as well as for the alleviation of flooding. Once the harbour was completed, the so-called *Fossa Traiana* seems to have acquired a function as a route to take barges up-river to Rome, while the northern canal remained primarily for flood relief.

The exact location chosen for construction of the Claudian harbour is difficult to understand, especially as it should be seen as a complement to the facilities at Ostia (Fig. 8.1). In the absence of a pre-existing harbour or settlement on the site, it would perhaps have made more sense to have built it closer to Ostia, either to the south of the Tiber mouth or immediately to its north. The more southerly location was presumably ruled out both because of a north-flowing coastal current and the density of occupation on this stretch of coast, which included a string of coastal villas belonging to prominent families (Lauro and Claridge 1998). Immediately to the north, currents around the river mouth may have been a problem.

The choice of the site may have been influenced not only by the availability of unoccupied land but also its particular characteristics. The geomorphological evidence suggests that the Claudian harbour basin and the associated port facilities were constructed to take advantage of the coastal dunes that lay between the sea and the salt-marshes behind (see above, p. 16 and Fig. 2.2). Cassius Dio seems to confirm this when he contrasts the part of the harbour excavated from the ground inland with that enclosed by the moles extending out to sea (**B1**). In order to capitalize on such a location without construction works being prone to danger from the flooding of the Tiber, the harbour had to be placed at the point where the course of the Tiber swings to the south. As well as removing the harbour from threat of the river inland, this also provided a larger site with greater space for development than was available closer to the river mouth. In this context, the early construction of the canals makes excellent sense, as they flank the construction site and so would have protected it from flooding whilst the inland portion of the harbour was being excavated. Nevertheless, the topography of the site for the new harbour was relatively constrained, limited to the coastal strip defined on the landward side by salt-marshes and lagoons.

Prior to the construction of the Claudian harbour, limitations on the size of ships that could gain access to the river port of Ostia meant that goods were either transferred onto barges from sea-going ships lying offshore close to the mouth of the Tiber, or transshipped at Puteoli and transported in smaller vessels to the Tiber mouth (Rickman 1971: 6–7). Claudius's initiative in developing a new harbour is related to his reforms in the administration of the *annona* and the establishment of the offices of *procurator annonae Ostis* and *procurator portus Ostiensis* (Rickman 1980: 48), although recent evidence suggests that it was with the completion of the harbour under Nero that the system was fully established (Bruun 2002: 163–4). Against this background, it seems likely that the Claudian harbour originally was conceived as replacing the former practice of transshipment off the mouth of the Tiber, with a growing number of sea-going ships entering the new harbour to unload their cargoes ready for transport up-river to Rome. While understanding of the development of the Claudian port is still fragmentary (see above, pp. 272–8), the extensive outer basin was certainly in use during the principate of Claudius (**B3**). We assume that construction of the buildings in the area between the *Portico di Claudio* and the *Canale di Comunicazione Trasverso* was also begun, although with the inner basin, or *Darsena*, they may not have been completed until late in the reign of Nero, as this

work incorporates a late Neronian brick stamp (see above, pp. 276–7). The completion of the orthogonally planned area on either side of the *Canale di Comunicazione Trasverso* may have been achieved only by the early Flavian period, as it seems integral with the road to Ostia, which, on the south side of the *Fossa Traiana*, is dated to some time after AD 69 (above, p. 57). This implies a gradual evolution of the functions of Portus through the period from Claudius to the Flavians. In essence it may have taken 30 years to grow from a large haven to a fully-functioning port settlement. Notwithstanding this development in the functions of Portus, it should be noted that it remained administratively subordinate to Ostia until the second century AD, and only achieved urban status by the earlier fourth century.

We do not know how the transshipment of goods onto river barges was undertaken, but two hypotheses can be explored. Firstly, we may envisage that goods were simply placed on barges drawn up beside the sea-going vessels in the outer basin of the Claudian harbour. This would have replicated the former process of transshipment used for vessels at anchor off the mouth of the Tiber but in a much more sheltered environment. Such large-scale transshipment would account for the huge size (*c.* 80 ha) of the outer basin. This kind of arrangement was probably used, at least until the port facilities were completed in the late 60s AD. It may account for the catastrophic loss of 200 ships in a violent storm within a harbour, presumed to be that at Portus, in AD 62 (**B7**). Rickman (1971: 11) concluded that the ships lost were probably the lighters used to transport the grain up-river. Once the construction of the harbour was completed, barges were also presumably berthed in the inner harbour, or *Darsena*, with the area of the future *Grandi Magazzini di Traiano* on its north side becoming a key storage and transshipment area. However, two factors suggest that the earlier process probably continued alongside this one. Firstly, the *Darsena* is limited in size, with quays totalling *c.* 440 m in length. This compares with a medium sized ship at *c.* 20–30 m, and the largest vessels perhaps up to 55 m (Casson 1971: 184–90). This implies that some goods would have continued to be directly transferred from ships to barges. Secondly, the process of transferring goods from ship to warehouse to barge was less efficient than moving them directly from ship to barge if they were to be moved up-river immediately. This suggests that whatever provision of warehousing there may have been around the *Darsena*, it was not concerned simply with transshipment but rather with the control, storage and regulation of commodities. In consequence, warehousing at the harbourside also provided a mechanism that allowed the flow of goods up the Tiber to be maintained at a steady rate throughout the year, rather than being determined by the irregular and highly seasonal pattern of the arrival and unloading of ships.

The route by which river barges entered the Tiber is also debatable. One suggestion is that, whilst the port was under construction, barge traffic bound for Rome exited from the main entrance of the outer basin of the Claudian harbour, turning south and entering the mouth of the Tiber and travelling to Rome via Ostia. In this way, the earlier practice of running barges from ships at anchor off the mouth of the river would have been replicated, only with the ships now protected by the moles within the new harbour. This suggestion is supported by the earlier observation that flood control during the construction of the new port was the primary function of the canals, since the epigraphic evidence makes no mention of their use for transport. The difficulty with this hypothesis for any period beyond the initial period of construction is that it proposes a cumbersome system that required barges to run against the current and negotiate the short stretch of sea between the Claudian harbour and the mouth of the Tiber, which may have become congested. Moreover, this stretch of river was also treacherous. However, it can also be argued that down to the late Neronian period, when the *Darsena* was completed, traffic would have had to approach the Tiber via the harbour mouth, either entering the sea exit of the *Fossa Traiana* or travelling by way of Ostia. Thereafter, traffic bound for Ostia would have continued to take this route. Some of that heading directly to Rome would have continued to enter the sea exit of the *Fossa Traiana* but most probably moved from the outer basin, past the *Darsena*, through the *Canale di Comunicazione Trasverso* and into the *Fossa Traiana*, and then up the Tiber. A drawback of the latter route is that the *Canale di Comunicazione Trasverso* forms an awkward angle of intersection with the *Fossa Traiana*, making it difficult to manoeuvre (see below, p. 301). Whichever route was used, the increased volume of traffic probably meant that there was always a threat of congestion on the river, a problem that can have been alleviated only by regulating the flow of goods. The development of warehousing will have aided in this, while the use of the canal to take barges to the Tiber will have relieved congestion at Ostia and at the Tiber mouth.

This then raises the question of the role of the new harbour in relation to the existing river port of Ostia. If it was originally conceived of as a supplementary transshipment centre, then although it needed its own facilities for the control of goods being unloaded, certain cargoes may have continued to pass through Ostia. This may suggest a degree of complementarity in the provision of warehouses at Ostia and Portus. As Rickman has noted (1971: 7), warehousing facilities at Ostia were extended during the first two centuries AD, a development that may be explained by the increasing volumes of shipping, both direct to Ostia and via Portus.

Attempts have been made previously to estimate the changing size of warehouses at Ostia on the basis of excavated evidence (Vitelli 1980). These data have been replicated taking measurements from the *Atlante di Ostia Antica* (Mannucci 1995). The excavated evidence is not complete and current work, which has already added to our knowledge of the river port, may yet reveal further warehouses (Heinzelmann and Martin 2002), not least because recent work has shown that the ancient port extended well beyond the Republican walls (Kockel 2001: fig. 3). Equally, although there are disputes about the identification of some buildings as *horrea*, the data can be considered to be reasonably reliable (Table 9.1). The evidence from Portus is less so, despite the new information from our survey. Our identification of certain buildings as *horrea*, and attempts to date them, have not been subject to the same close scrutiny as the evidence from Ostia. Furthermore, Claudian warehouses may have been obliterated by the construction of the hexagon of the Trajanic harbour. The sizes of some buildings are uncertain, while there is also good reason to believe that several of them had more than one floor given over to warehousing (Rickman 1971: 129–30). This means that the estimated sizes of the buildings given in Table 9.1 should be used only to provide a general order of magnitude.

Nevertheless, comparison of *horrea* at Portus with those from Ostia reveals some important differences. First, although only a few warehouses at Portus can definitely be assigned a Claudian date, they cover almost twice the area of those identified at Ostia. With the exception of the so-called *Foro Olitorio* at Portus (see below, p. 304), the buildings at both sites lie in the same size range. This does not suggest any significant distinction in function. However, unlike Ostia, where *horrea* tend to be situated close to the Tiber on the north side of the town (Rickman 1971: fig. 1), those at

Portus cluster around the *Darsena* in the core of the port, but are absent in the area beside the large outer basin. It is certainly clear that by the time that the first-century port was completed, the scale of operation at Portus was greater than that at Ostia, perhaps with differentiation between the kinds of cargo that each handled. This is a corrective to the view that there was little or no warehousing at Portus prior to the construction of the Trajanic harbour (see above, p. 38; *pace* Rickman 2002: 357). In sum, the continued growth of warehousing facilities at Ostia probably points to an overall increase in the volume of cargo entering both ports, with Portus complementing Ostia, rather than eclipsing it. It is equally clear that the development of Portus in the first century did not result in any decline at Puteoli (see above, pp. 37–8). Alexandrian corn ships continued to dock there in the later first century (Rickman 1980: 75) and the archaeological evidence from the town demonstrates that it was very prosperous well into the second century (De Caro 2002).

However the harbour at Portus worked during the Claudian and Neronian periods, it is clear that it was regularly planned, since the *Darsena*, the colonnaded road to its south, the *Portico di Claudio*, the *Foro Olitorio* and the *Canale di Comunicazione Trasverso* all conform to an orthogonal plan (**Fig. 8.2**). Equally, the outer harbour basin appears to have been planned around an axis perpendicular to this, which was marked by the lighthouse and a line of lanterns (see above, p. 275). By contrast, the *Fossa Traiana* runs at a different angle, probably because it was built earlier in the sequence of development, and was laid out roughly parallel to the northern Claudian canal, before the whole of the port complex was planned.

The orthogonal layout of the port suggests that the approaches from both land and sea influenced its design. The centrality of the approach by sea is emphasized architecturally by the façades of the port overlooking the harbour, which are best seen in the surviving portions of the *Portico di Claudio* (**Fig. 9.2**). The landward approaches are more difficult to assess. A traditional view would suggest that the main approach from Rome was along the Via Campana, which had led down the valley to the salterns in the region since the Republican period. The recently excavated stretch of this road near Ponte Galeria shows that it was reconstructed in the early first century AD (above, p. 58; Pietraggi *et al.* 2001). Since no trace of the road has been found in the survey, we conclude that as it approached Portus it ran below what is now the Tiber

embankment, and then followed the *Fossa Traiana* and entered the port area from the east, beside the early aqueduct, and not far distant from where tombs of Flavian date were discovered by Calza (1925: 60–5; **Fig. 8.2**). However important this road may have been, its alignment does not seem to have influenced the layout of the orthogonal grid.

The second land route to Portus approached from Ostia to the south, by the road later known as the Via Flavia (**Fig. 8.2**). The history of this road is uncertain (see above, p. 278), but there is no firm evidence for its existence prior to the earlier Flavian period. Taken at face value, this suggests that it was created as a result of the growing need to facilitate the movement of officials and other personnel between the river port and Portus during this period. However, it seems inconceivable that Ostia and Portus were not connected by land from the outset. Although it could be argued that such a link was provided by a towpath along the Tiber, this indirect route does not seem very likely. Alternatively, we can hypothesize that the Via Flavia had an antecedent.

An earlier alignment for the predecessor of the Via Flavia may be preserved in the road running parallel and to the west of the *Canale di Comunicazione Trasverso* on the north side of the *Fossa Traiana*. This street is integral to the orthogonal plan and would have formed a key intersection with the east–west colonnaded road to the south side of the *Darsena*. On this basis, it could be argued that the approach from Ostia was axial to the planning of first-century Portus. In this respect, we may note how the *Canale di Comunicazione Traverso* is centrally placed between the line of the *Portico di Claudio* to the west and a southward projection of the line of the *Molo Destro* to the east. This raises the prospect that the awkward angle of intersection between the north–south *Canale di Comunicazione Traverso* and the *Fossa Traiana* was determined by the adherence of the north–south canal to this grid. Such a design would have emphasized the intimate relationship of Portus's connection to Ostia.

If we take the plan as symmetrical about the axis of the *Canale di Comunicazione Traverso*, then tentatively we can restore the plan as a block of buildings bisected by this canal and flanking the south side of the harbour basin (**Fig. 8.2**). This suggests that the settlement occupied a zone *c.* 750×300 m, covering approximately 22.5 ha — less than one-third of the area of early Imperial Ostia. Such a grid plan is characteristic of contemporary urban foundations, particularly colonies in the provinces (Gros and Torelli

TABLE 9.1.   Comparison of areas occupied by horrea at Portus and Ostia.

Site	Area	Building	Date	Type	Area (m²)	First century (m²)	Early second century (m²)	Later second century (m²)
OSTIA	I.VII	Piccolo Mercato	Hadrianic	courtyard	1,204		1,204	
	I.VIII.1	Horrea	c. 120	courtyard	3,841		3,841	
	I.VIII.2	Horrea	119–20	courtyard	1,950		1,950	
	I.VIII.3	Horrea Epagathiana et Epaphroditiana	145–50	courtyard	1,036			1,036
	I.XIII.1	Horrea	Trajanic–Hadrianic	courtyard	405		405	
	I.XIX.4		Trajanic	courtyard	2,072		2,072	
	I.XX		Trajanic	courtyard			0	
	II.II.7	Horrea Antoniniana	Late Antonine	?courtyard	13,200			13,200
	II.IX.7	Grandi Horrea	mid-first century	courtyard	8,667	8,667		
	III.II.6	Horrea	Trajanic	corridor	432		432	
	III.XVII.1	Horrea	Trajanic–Hadrianic	corridor	495		495	
	III.XVII		Trajanic	courtyard			0	
	IV.V.12	Horrea	Augustan	corridor	360	360		
	IV.VIII		Hadrianic	corridor	1,386		1,386	
	V.I.2		Claudian	courtyard	2,760	2,760		
	V.XI.8	Horrea dell'Artemide	Trajanic	courtyard	2,430		2,430	
	V.XII.1	Horrea di Hortensis	mid-first century	courtyard	5,880	5,880		
	no. = 17			Total new		17,667	14,215	14,236
				Total	46,118	1,7667	31,882	46,118
				Average		4,416.75	1,579	7,118
PORTUS	Darsena	South of Darsena	Claudian?	corridor	3,375	3,375		
	Darsena	Foro Olitorio	Claudian?	courtyard	23,715	23,715		
	Darsena	Grandi Magazzini Traiano	Claudian?	corridor	5,700	5,700		
	Side V"	6.6	Trajanic	spine	2,700		2,700	
	SideV'	Grandi Magazzini di Settimio Severo	later second century	corridor	51,165			51,165

Site	Area	Building	Date	Type	Area (m²)	First century (m²)	Early second century (m²)	Later second century (m²)
	Side VI	8.2	Trajanic	courtyard	936		936	
	Side VI	8.3	Trajanic	courtyard	643.5		643.5	
	Side VI	8.4	Trajanic	courtyard	994.5		994.5	
	Side VI	8.11	Trajanic	courtyard	1,782		1,782	
	Side VI	8.12	Trajanic	courtyard	968		968	
	Side VI	8.13	Trajanic	courtyard	880		880	
	Side VI	9.1	Trajanic	corridor	2,247		2,247	
	Side VI	9.2	Trajanic	corridor	1,836		1,836	
	Side VI	9.3	Trajanic	corridor	1,710		1,710	
	Side VI	9.4	Trajanic	corridor	1,624.5		1,624.5	
	Side III	11.2	Trajanic	spine	5,591.25		5,591.25	
	Side III	11.3	Trajanic	spine	3,150		3,150	
	Side III	11.7	Trajanic	spine	2,925		2,925	
	Side III	11.8	Trajanic	spine	1,800		1,800	
	Side III	Two others uncertain						
	Side II	12.6/7	Trajanic	spine	4,950		4,950	
	Side II	12.2	Trajanic	spine	4,950		4,950	
	Side II	12.3	Trajanic	spine	4,950		4,950	
	Side II	Another the same?	Trajanic		4,950		4,950	
	Side I	Based on Lanciani	Trajanic	spine?	4,950		4,950	
	Side I	Based on Lanciani	Trajanic	spine	4,950		4,950	
	Riverside	A12	later second century? +	courtyard	346.5			346.5
		A36	later second century? +	corridor?	472.5			472.5
		A37	later second century? +	courtyard	810			810
	no. = 29			Total new		32,790	59,488	52,794
				Total	145,072	32,790	92,278	145,072
				Average		10,930	2,832.75	13,198.5

41

FIG. 9.2. **The *Portico di Claudio*** from the south as seen today. *(Photo: Martin Millett.)*

1988: 265–388; Sommella 1988: 227–50). Thus, although there are no direct parallels for the design of the Claudian harbour, clearly it can be related to urban planning, although this does contrast with the apparent absence of a focal public building complex.

The administrative dependence of Portus upon Ostia is reinforced by the absence of firm epigraphic or structural evidence for public buildings, major cults or housing prior to the second century AD. The only major building that appears to originate in this period is the so-called *Foro Olitorio*. In the foregoing discussion, we have assumed that this was a large warehouse, as it falls within the category of courtyard *horrea* described by Rickman (1971). Nevertheless, its position at the core of the port may suggest that it had a different function. In addition, it should be noted that this complex faced directly onto the *Fossa Traiana* rather than being connected to the *Darsena* to the north. Its plan is not dissimilar to some *macella* (Gros 1996: 450–64), or even the Piazzale delle Corporazione at Ostia (Pavolini 1989: 68), but its substantially larger size distinguishes it. Another possibility, that it is a forum, seems unlikely, as there is no evidence for any associated temple and the port lacked a civic constitution at this period.

Very little is known of the pre-Trajanic phase of the so-called *Palazzo Imperiale*, making it impossible to assess whether the buildings in this area fulfilled any official function. Although the function of the circular building (structure 8.15) in this area remains uncertain, it appears focal to the harbour design. There is no evidence to suggest that there was an imperial palace here, and Pliny's account of a visit from Claudius during construction provides the only direct evidence for an imperial presence at Portus in this period (**B3**).

It is evident from a range of sources that the construction of the Claudian harbour and the associated canals was an imperial project from which both Claudius and Nero derived considerable kudos. In addition to Claudius's visit to the site during its construction, Nero commemorated its inauguration on a special coin issue (**Fig. 9.3**). It involved engineering work on a massive scale, details of which are reported by a number of ancient writers (**B1**, **B2**, **B4** and **B6**). By implication, it also represents a very substantial investment of capital and materials. The boldness and sweep of its architectural conception is evident in the design of the *Portico di Claudio* and the colonnaded road to the south of the *Darsena*, as well as in the scale of the *Foro Olitorio*. Similarly, the famous inscription that commemorates the inauguration of the canals during the construction of the port (**A1**) clearly adorned an imperial monument of some size (**Fig. 9.1**), possibly a monumental arch (see above, p. 36).

All of this suggests that the Claudian harbour made an important statement about the imperial power to seaborne travellers approaching Rome, as well as those arriving overland. It was also clearly a project that was

FIG. 9.3. The reverse of a coin of Nero minted in AD 64 (A2; *RIC* I, 178–83) commemorating the construction of the harbour at Portus. *(Photo: Adi Popescu.)*

the Claudian harbour as a massive, functional extension to the established town and river port of Ostia or simply 'a harbour of refuge' (Rickman 2002: 357). We should take care also to consider it in the context of contemporary imperial building programmes, which give as much emphasis to public utility as elaborate display. Portus and Ostia were intimately related and had complementary roles, but the Claudian harbour was distinguished in its judicious and artificially engineered blend of functionality and imperial grandeur rather than by elaborate artistic embellishment.

THE TRAJANIC HARBOUR

There can be little doubt that the Claudian harbour continued to develop considerably during the half century after its inception. Evidence for this does not come readily from the survey results, but can be gleaned from other published sources. Several brick-built tombs of Flavian date were discovered beneath the southern end of the Trajanic warehouses on side III of the hexagon (Calza 1925: 60–6). One of these belonged to a *tabularius* of the *Portus Augusti*, attesting the presence of officials and the existence of a settled community at the port (Calza 1925: 64; *CIL* XIV suppl. 4482). Recent excavations beneath the *Basilica Portuense* confirm that occupation in this central part of the settlement was well underway by the early Flavian period (see above, pp. 258–9). Additionally, the development of a *statio marmorum* on the southern bank of the *Fossa Traiana* by the reign of Domitian (Pensabene 2002: 27) signals the increasing importance of this canal for barge traffic going up the Tiber to Rome. Finally, growing use of the road from Ostia to Portus from the early Flavian period stimulated the subsequent growth of a small community on the southern bank of the *Fossa Traiana*. If we can envisage the original plan for the harbour as initially having been as a northern extension of Ostia, then we see the new facility operating more independently from the AD 60s onwards. Nevertheless, the structural axis of the port remained determined by a north–south alignment.

Construction of the Trajanic harbour represents a reaffirmation of the growing importance of the port. It was probably a result of a conscious decision that Portus should replace Puteoli as the destination for the

much discussed by the literate classes at Rome at the time, as is evidenced by the accounts surrounding the construction of the lighthouse (**B1** and **B6**).

By contrast, there is surprisingly little evidence for architectural decoration or sculpture. The sculpture and epigraphy provide little evidence of first-century dedications. Amongst the portraits there are only two, both Julio-Claudian, while there are also only two inscriptions, one Claudian (**A1**), the other to Divus Vespasianus (Tables **9.2** and **9.3**; see also below, p. 311). Indeed, this stands in marked contrast to the richness of embellishment in the contemporary port city of Puteoli, which remained a key centre of trade and imperial patronage until at least the second century (De Caro 2002: 70–9). The paucity of evidence at Portus may not be surprising, given the longevity of the port's use, its periodic despoliation since the early medieval period (Bignamini 2004), the burial of much of the first-century site beneath later buildings, and destruction caused by the construction of the Trajanic hexagonal basin. This means we should be careful not to dismiss

TABLE 9.2. Sculptural evidence from Portus.

	Reference in Lugli and Filibeck 1935	Edition of Museo Torlonia Catalogue cited by Lugli and Filibeck 1935 (Visconti 1880)	Edition of Museo Torlonia Catalogue in British School at Rome library (Visconti 1883)
IMPERIAL PORTRAIT BUSTS AND STATUES			
Tiberius	p. 166	no. 349	-
Claudius (?)	p. 166, fig. 91	no. 249	no. 238
Hadrian	p. 166, fig. 94	no. 546	no. 456
Matidia	p. 166, fig. 93	no. 544	-
Marcus Aurelius	p. 166	no. 367	-
Faustina II	p. 166	no. 245	no. 235
Commodus	p. 166	no. 364	-
Didius Julianus	p. 166	no. 562	-
Septimius Severus	p. 166, fig. 92	no. 136	no. 136
Caracalla	p. 166, fig. 95	no. 568	no. 477
Severus Alexander	p. 166	no. 365	-
Aurelian	p. 166	no. 607	no. 515
Mariniana	p. 167	no. 603	no. 511
DEITIES			
Aesculapius	p. 165	no. 94	-
Ammon (Clipeus)	p. 166-67	no. 287	-
Ammon (Herm)	p. 166	no. 466	no. 374
Apollo	p. 165, fig. 83	no. 370	no. 282
Bacchus (Herm)	p. 166	-	-
Diana Huntress	p. 165	no. 366	-
Eros	p. 166	no. 171	-
Juno ?	p. 165, fig. 84	no. 184	-
Jupiter	p. 166, fig. 88	no. 400	-
Jupiter ?	p. 166	no. 399	no. 310
Minerva	p. 166, fig. 86	no. 298	no. 279
Minerva	p. 166, fig. 87	no. 183	-
Neptune	p. 166	no. 250	-
Poseidon	p. 165, fig. 6 in Lateran Collection, Vatican Museum	-	
Venus	p. 165	no. 4	-
Venus of Cnidus	p. 166, fig. 85	no. 146	-
MYTHOLOGICAL FIGURES			
Group of Fauns	p. 166	no. 116	-
Hercules and Telephus	p. 166	no. 388	no. 298
Leda and the swan	p. 166	no. 60	-
Orestes and Electra	p. 166	no. 95	-
Semi-naked male	p. 165	no. 8	-
MISCELLANEOUS PORTRAITS AND STATUES			
Pompey (?)	p. 166	no. 343	-
Ptolemy II	p. 166	no. 401	no. 316
Athlete	p. 166	no. 470	no. 380
Athlete	p. 166	no. 473	no. 386
Athlete	p. 166, fig. 89	no. 476	no. 383
Ephebe	p. 166, fig. 90	no. 355	-
Gazelle	p. 166	no. 452	no. 362
Lisia (Herm)	p. 166	no. 30	-
Puttus	p. 166	no. 436	-

TABLE 9.3. **Epigraphic evidence from Portus.**

	Latin inscriptions (Thylander 1952)	Greek inscriptions (Sacco 1984)
DEDICATIONS		
Claudius	B310	
Divus Vespasianus	B330	
Trajan	B311, B312, B313, B314, B315	
Antoninus Pius	B316, B317, B318	
Commodus	B296, B297, B301, B319	no. 2
Septimius Severus	B288, B292, B320	
Septimius Severus and Caracalla	B321	no. 4
Septimius Severus, Caracalla and Julia Domna		no. 3
Caracalla	B322	
Severus Alexander	B324	
Severus Alexander and Julia Mamea		no. 17
Gordian III		no. 5
Constantine, Licinus and Maximinus	B325	
Theodosius II and Valentinanus III	B327	
DEITY		
Diamones		no. 50
Diana Iobens	B287	
Fortuna	B288	
Hercules	B289, B292	
Isis	B293, B308	nos. 6, 18, 21
Jupiter Dolichenus	B296, B319	
Jupiter Heliopolitanus	B297	
Liber Pater	B298, B299, B300, B301, B306	no. 8
Magna Mater	B142, B308	
Mamas		nos. 5, 10
Minerva	B302	
Serapis	B304, B308	nos. 2, 3, 13, 14, 15, 16, 17, 19, 20, 21
Silvanus	B305, B306	
Sol Invictus	B307	
Vulcan	B304	no. 13
Zeus Helios	B304	

Alexandrian grain fleet (Rickman 2002: 357; see also above, p. 38), reflecting Trajan's broader reforms of the *annona* (Rickman 1980: 90). Although we have argued that there was a strong element of topographic continuity in the western half of the port, the construction of the hexagonal basin to its east and the provision of a road and canal directly connecting the whole complex with the Tiber enhanced its established links with Rome. This represents something of a realignment of the axis of the port.

The location of the hexagon is understood easily in terms of the existing topography. Specifically, its western side is parallel to the Claudian grid and there was presumably advantage in maintaining this

conformity. More generally, its position seems to have taken advantage of the lagoon and salt-marshes that lay behind the coastal strip upon which the Claudian harbour had been constructed. These presumably provided relatively soft, low-lying ground within which to excavate the enormous basin. The hexagon most likely impinged on the eastern edge of the earlier settlement, but left the pre-existing harbour basins free, thus enabling the port to continue in use during the period of construction.

The overall plan of the Trajanic complex is certainly unique and, unlike the Claudian development, it is difficult to find any parallels for it in urban planning. Indeed, even contemporary harbour developments like

Centumcellae provide no comparisons (Caruso 1991: 34–9; Torelli 1993: 112–15). Its most distinctive feature is the hexagonal basin. This design has no precedent in ancient harbour design (Blackman 1982a; 1982b), although the concept of building an inland harbour basin artificially emulating the natural bays, used at places like Baiae (Scognamiglio 2001: tav. 1) and Misenum (De Caro and Greco 1993: 66), does have parallels, for instance at Carthage (Hurst 1994: 45–8) or at Seleucia in Peria (Van Berchem 1985: carte 1). However, both the scale and the shape of the hexagon of the Trajanic harbour are without precedent. It has been suggested that the rectangular harbour at Carthage was modified to create a hexagonal form (Stager 1992: 76–7), but the evidence for this has been questioned by Hurst (1999: 19). Even if the Carthage basin was modified to be hexagonal, the dating suggests that it was emulating Portus and not a model for it.

Juvenal (**B11**) clearly talks about Portus but without explicit reference to its hexagonal shape, and the only direct ancient reference to this is the commemorative coin issued by the emperor Trajan (**A3**; **Fig. 9.4**). There has, therefore, been considerable debate as to why a hexagonal shape should have been chosen. Lugli (Lugli and Filibeck 1935: 35–6) suggested that it was dictated in part by the pre-existing structures of the Claudian port, not least the mole and baths along the north side of what was to become the *Canale di Imbocco del Porto di Traiano*, as well as the area of the *Palazzo Imperiale* (Lugli and Filibeck 1935: tav. III nos. 8, 9, 11, 13, 14). He also suggested that the southern limit of the hexagonal basin was predetermined by the Claudian canal that he believed preceded much of the line of the *Fossa Traiana* (although our evidence disproves this — see above, pp. 276–7). In terms of function, he believed that the hexagon would have facilitated the transshipment of cargoes onto barges for transport to the docks at Rome. The arguments of Meiggs (1973: 162) and Testaguzza (1970: 55) ran on similar lines, although the former added that the hexagonal shape would also have been useful for the distribution of shipping and warehouses (see also Zevi 2000a: 519), while the latter suggested that it would have readily lent itself to the division of the wharves into sectors and the organization of arriving and departing fleets. Giuliani (1992: 42), however, suggested that any attempt to try and understand the hexagonal form solely in terms of an architect having designed something that 'fitted-in' with previous port structures was 'too reductive'.

The main problem in trying to understand the rationale behind the adoption of a hexagonal form is that we are used to seeing the basin in a way that contemporaries would never have seen it — in plan as from the air. There is little doubt that the hexagonal form may be explained in part by its aesthetic appeal to the Emperor Trajan and his architect, who might have been Apollodorus of Damascus (see above, p. 42 n. 37). Its novel architectural sophistication suggests that its elegant plan was as important as its impact on the ground. However, any workable explanation surely needs to take into account how the hexagonal space would have appeared to people using the harbour, as well as how it might have fitted in with the pre-existing topography, and facilitated berthing and transshipment.

A visit to the water-filled hexagon today reminds us that, wherever we stand, we do not have the impression that we are standing within a hexagonal space. Instead, the opposite two or three sides appear as a single continuous line, and it is very difficult to see the change of angle between one side and the next, although the buildings along the quayside in antiquity would perhaps have articulated and emphasized these corners. This stresses the importance of the design as it was to be seen and in this respect we should not neglect the impact that entry into the hexagon would have had on people sailing into it. They arrived through the outer basin of the Claudian harbour, passing the great lighthouse at its mouth, then approached the monumental structures along the southern side of the basin before entering the *Canale di Imbocco del Porto di Traiano*. This would have been hemmed in by the great warehouses and surrounding porticoes, and on turning they would have seen the colossal statue of Trajan, the temple and surrounding enclosure at the centre of side II lying directly ahead. Entering the hexagon, this complex would have appeared as the central point of an almost continuous maritime façade, composed of the frontages of the warehouses and other buildings that framed the basin. This itself will have created a theatrical approach appropriate to Rome's power, almost a miniature of the landlocked Mediterranean sea itself. The commemorative *sestertius* of Trajan captures something of the sense of this (**Fig. 9.4**). The image on its reverse side has the buildings along sides I, III, IV and VI of the hexagon skewed to emphasize those on side II, where the colossal statue of Trajan and the temple were located, even though they are not shown.

In addition to this, there are also a number of practical considerations that might have contributed to

FIG. 9.4. **The reverse of a coin issue dated** AD 103–11 (A3; *RIC* II, no. 471) **showing the hexagonal harbour at Portus.** *(Photo: Soprintendenza per i Beni Archeologici di Ostia.)*

the choice of a hexagonal shape. The form does have the functional advantage of a high ratio of quayside length to basin area and added *c.* 2 km to the quays available in the complex. This readily lent itself to the accommodation of large numbers of ships, with the berths on each side being separated by sequentially numbered columns. The shape also allowed further ships to be moored towards the centre of the basin whilst awaiting a berth. At the same time, analysis of structures on each of the sides suggests that there were differences in function that were enhanced by the shape of the basin. Side V provided access from the basin to the *Canale di Imbocco del Porto di Traiano* and thence the *Canale di Comunicazione Trasverso* and the *Darsena*. Side VI comprises an integrated complex of courtyard *horrea* and perhaps also provided an administrative focus at the so-called *Palazzo Imperiale*. Side I seems to have been for storage alone. Side II was the ideological focus for the complex, also providing extensive storage facilities, and it gave access towards the Tiber along the Via Portuense. Side III was a key transshipment point between the hexagon and the canal that ran eastwards to the Tiber. It also had access towards the Tiber by way of the Via

Portuense. The warehouses on side IV also screened the apparent residential areas to the south and west. All of this suggests that the hexagonal shape may have been chosen in part because it promoted functional differentiation between areas for storage, transshipment and redistribution, therefore facilitating control over the movement of cargoes.

The genius of the hexagonal shape is surely, therefore, that it fulfilled all of these functions, both practical and ideological, whilst at the same time fitting into the pre-existing topography of the Claudio-Neronian harbour, so that it could continue to function during the decade or so needed for its construction (see above, p. 307). Rickman, however, has pointed out that this shape would have 'created complicated L-shaped links between harbours, and from the inner harbour to the *Fossa Traiana*, which must have necessitated ships being towed or winched by capstans, from one area to another' (1996: 289).

The other major new addition to the port was the *c.* 35 m wide canal that connects the earlier *Fossa Traiana* with the Tiber, running parallel with side III of the hexagon before curving eastwards towards the river. Its purpose seems to have been primarily one of transshipment, facilitating the movement of goods that had been either unloaded from sea-going ships in the hexagon or held in the adjacent warehouses before being transferred to barges moored along the canal. This probably now became a principal route of communication for barges moving between Portus and the Tiber. We may note that the largest of the barges excavated in the Claudian harbour in 1959 (Fiumicino 2) had an estimated total length of *c.* 22 m and beam of *c.* 5 m (Scrinari 1979: 43). Such vessels would have been of an appropriate size to use this canal, supporting the suggestion that these vessels were used to move goods up the Tiber from Portus to Rome (Boetto 2001a: 125). The canal was flanked by broad towpaths raised above the surrounding landscape and accessed at intervals by steps (cf. **Fig. 8.5**). It is likely that this canal is that commemorated on a contemporary inscription (**A4**). It may also be that to which Pliny the Younger refers (**B13**), incidentally showing that the canals were still considered important for the relief of periodic flooding by the Tiber. The *Fossa Traiana* also continued in use, certainly for the transport of marble from the *statio marmorum* on the Isola Sacra, up to the Tiber and thence up-river to Rome.

These developments enhanced direct contact up-river to Rome, but it seems highly unlikely that the warehouse and canalside quays on side III had sufficient capacity to cope with all the goods brought into the hexagon. It is not clear how goods unloaded on the remaining sides of the hexagonal basin were transshipped. Goods were presumably unloaded from the ships directly into the warehouses for longer-term storage rather than immediate transshipment. When needed, goods in the warehouse around the other sides of the hexagon were presumably most often loaded onto barges at the adjacent quays and then transported out of the hexagon via the *Canale di Comunicazione Trasverso* and the *Fossa Traiana* to the Tiber. Alternatively, some may have been moved along the roads around the hexagon to the canal, where they were loaded onto barges to travel to Rome via the *Fossa Traiana*, while other barges may have continued to use the sea-route to Ostia.

Construction of the hexagonal basin by Trajan also enabled the number of warehouses at Portus to be greatly increased. The total amount of storage capacity increased to over 90,000 m^2, some three times the capacity of those known at Ostia (Table 9.1). Even though new warehouses had also been built at the river port, they were on average less than half the size of those at Portus. Moreover, the types of buildings differ. At Ostia the dominant form is the courtyard type, whilst at Portus all are corridor forms, with the exceptions of the *Foro Olitorio*, perhaps the *Grandi Magazzini di Settimio Severo*, and a series of courtyard buildings on side VI of the hexagon (Table 9.1). Finally, although there was some preference for the *horrea* at Ostia to be positioned close to the river, they continued to permeate the city (Meiggs 1973: fig. 24). By contrast, the warehousing at Portus concentrates around the *Darsena* and the hexagon.

The scale and form of warehouses at Portus signify control of commodities. This is evident from the way that the corridor *horrea* were enclosed (Rickman 1971: 126; 2002: 357), and the fact that they were accessed from the hexagon by relatively small openings in the *Contramura Interne*. Moreover, the majority lack the central courtyard characteristic of many *horrea* at Ostia and indeed most of those in the emporium at Rome (Aguilera Martín 2002: 51–104). Since these presumably were used as a place for negotiation and trading between individuals,[2] their frequency at Ostia and absence at Portus further underlines the distinction between the two centres. It could be argued that these patterns reflect the dominance of state-controlled

transport at Portus, in contrast with smaller-scale private entrepreneurial activity at Ostia. Nevertheless, it should be acknowledged that the distinction between these two forms of activity may have been rather less sharp than this implies. Another explanation for the distinctions observed may lie in the role of the *horrea* at Portus for the longer-term storage of bulk foodstuffs, with their dispatch to Rome as and when needed, regulating the flow of barges up the Tiber (see above, pp. 299–300). In this sense, the warehouses at Portus should perhaps not be compared with those at Ostia but instead should be seen as unique, acting as the reservoir of food for Rome (Fig. 9.5).

The resolution of the survey evidence makes it difficult to characterize differences between *horrea*, but they are sufficiently clear to suggest variations in function on different sides of the hexagon. *Horrea* of the corridor-type predominate on all but side VI, where there are sets of courtyard buildings. However, there are variations in the styles of the form of corridor buildings, with the rooms mostly either *c.* 6 m or *c.* 8 m in width. Moreover, the presence and form of the surrounding corridors differ between buildings. While it might in theory be possible to relate some of these differences to particular commodities, this lies beyond the scope of the present study. Grain was a key commodity stored at the harbour; floors raised on *suspensurae* have definitely been identified in the warehouses excavated by Calza (1925: 58–60) along side III and were certainly present in others.

In the area to the east of the hexagon, the new Trajanic canal stimulated development, most noticeably along its northern side and close to the point where it joined the Tiber. In neither area are the buildings as monumental as those around the hexagon, and it is probable that we should view them as the result of entrepreneurial activity around the margins of the port. The buildings lying beside the canal resemble warehouses or workshops, with quays to provide access to the water. The settlement by the Tiber presumably indicates the importance of this route and junction, and facilities were developed to allow people to get on and off river boats going to either Rome or Ostia. In the settlement by the side of the Tiber, there are three small *horrea* and presumably also facilities for disembarkation and loading. Significantly, the *horrea* are comparatively small and, like those at Ostia, two are of courtyard form (Table 9.1).

The survey has also made an important contribution to the understanding of the range of buildings present at the Trajanic port. The temple and its precinct in the

FIG. 9.5. **The southeast frontage of the** *Grandi Magazzini di Settimio Severo* **from the southwest.** *(Photo: Martin Millett.)*

middle of side II of the hexagon, apparently dedicated to Liber Pater, lay opposite the entrance to the basin and was clearly an important monumental focus. Its precise character, however, remains unclear. While it is true that the well-known mid-second-century AD dedicatory inscription to P. Lucilius Gamala (*iunior*) mentions his benefactions to the forum and temples, and is recorded as having been found 'nel Foro Portuense' (Thylander 1952: B335), it has been shown clearly that this munificence benefited Ostia rather than Portus (Meiggs 1973: 493–502; D'Arms 2000). Aside from the *Tempio di Portuno* and the *Palazzo Imperiale*, the function of both of which still remains unclear, there is little physical evidence for public buildings. The survey did not cover the site of Lanciani's supposed temple between the *Episcopio* and the

Canale di Comunicazione Trasverso, or the *Horrea Terme* on Monte Giulio. Apart from the temple in the middle of side II of the hexagon, our only other evidence consists of the various temples referred to by inscriptions or indicated by statuary (Tables 9.2 and 9.3), but their material remains have not been identified. In the area to the east of the hexagon, where the Trajanic canal meets the Tiber, however, aerial photographs revealed the remains of several buildings interpreted as temples. These may have marked the junction between canal, road and Tiber, as a point of transition either between the land and the water, or between the living and the dead (see below, p. 312).

The inscriptions and sculptural evidence (Tables 9.2 and 9.3) indicate a rich and diverse range of religious practice and imperial connections at the port itself, and excavations have uncovered an Isaeum on the Isola Sacra on the southern side of the *Fossa Traiana* (Lauro 1993: 170–2). It is notable that there is strong evidence not only for oriental cults, as well as Judaism and Christianity, but also the presence of an Alexandrian community at the port (Sacco 1984). In the absence of large-scale excavated evidence, their chronology can be established only broadly. However, Zevi (2000a: 512–14) has related the establishment of the cult of Serapis at Ostia in the early second century (prior to AD 127) to the first arrival of the Alexandrian grain fleet at Portus. It is also notable that the imperial dedications and sculptures of members of the imperial house are mostly of second- to third-century date. It is remarkable, in particular, that after the peak in dedications of Trajanic date the list of inscriptions only continues with Antoninus Pius, and then remains strong to the mid-third century. The portraiture shows a similar overall pattern.

There is little doubt that the use of the new hexagonal basin and its facilities would have required a substantially increased labour force. Meiggs (1973: 534) suggested that by the Severan period, the port may have had a population of several thousand. Although there is no specific evidence to support this figure, it is true that the scale of activities at the port was now far greater than it had been before. Epigraphic evidence attests a range of activities and the existence of various *collegia* at Portus (Lugli and Filibeck 1935: 138–43), while there would also have been facilities for travellers, like the later second-century military recruit from Egypt who wrote home to say that he was in Portus awaiting assignment to his unit (*P. Mich*. VIII, 490). The geophysical survey of Portus means that for the first time there is more justification for attempting to locate the main areas of residential settlement. This would seem to lie in the relatively compact area between the *Canale di Comunicazione Trasverso*, side V of the hexagon and the *Fossa Traiana*. Here the geophysical survey points to the existence of buildings that cannot be identified easily, but are certainly not *horrea*. Excavations in the vicinity of the later *Basilica Portuense* show that this area, which was first developed in the first century AD, remained a residential focus for the port (see above, pp. 258–65). It is also likely that there was further residential settlement on the west side of the *Canale di Comunicazione Trasverso*, although here the evidence is more equivocal. Notwithstanding these indications, there is no clear evidence for tenement blocks similar to those at Ostia, or for a large domus, in any part of the port or beside the Tiber. Only in the area of intensive occupation to the north of the *Basilica Portuense* is there evidence that is perhaps consistent with the presence of such buildings. Although some of the population may have lived in the upper floors of the warehouses, definitive evidence for this is lacking. The only possible major residential building is the *Palazzo Imperiale*, although details of this remain unclear. As argued in the discussion of the pre-Trajanic period, it seems unlikely that this was an imperial residence (Fig. 9.6). Although there is no direct evidence that Trajan or any of his successors stopped at Portus when leaving or arriving at Rome (Spurza 2002), this may be because it was such a commonplace event as not to be considered worth recording by contemporary sources. Indeed, the inscription that prays for the safe return of Septimius Severus, Caracalla and Julia Domna from Egypt in AD 199–200 (Sacco 1984: no. 3) surely implies that they travelled via Portus. However, the *Palazzo Imperiale* does not seem large enough or sufficiently accessible within the port to have acted as the temporary residence of the emperor, or as the setting of an imperial *adventus*. It seems most likely that the building enjoyed some other function, perhaps official.

One characteristic of the site revealed by the survey is the large extent of its cemeteries. Extensive areas of burial have been identified in the area beside the Tiber and in the zone to the north of the Trajanic aqueduct.

In the first of these areas, excavations in the 1970s at Stalla-Buoi revealed tombs furnished with rich sarcophagi of the third century AD, while other such fragments have been recovered in our field walking (see above, pp. 193–201). Evidence from nineteenth-century excavations in the vicinity of the *Tempio di Portuno* show that in the late antique period burial extended further to the west, around the *Mura Costantiniane*. It is also possible that the *Tempio di Portuno* was constructed as a mausoleum (see above, p. 290). Late burials have also been excavated elsewhere within the port complex (Coccia 1996: 300–1 fig. 2). The overall impression is of large-scale cemeteries dating from the first century AD onwards. This, together with the evidence of the cemeteries on the Isola Sacra (Calza 1940; Baldassare 2001), implies that Portus had a very substantial resident population and a broad social spectrum.

This contrasts with Ostia where, notwithstanding the size of the town, cemeteries are relatively scarce, and this may imply that some of the Portus cemeteries served both communities, again emphasizing the close links between them. It is notable that the earliest attested funerary structures at Portus are along the side of the Tiber (Fig. 5.50). It is clear that these monumental tombs were designed to be seen from the river, and as such they may relate primarily to Ostia rather than Portus. The riverside location clearly parallels the well-known pattern of tombs lining the roads approaching Roman towns. We may note also that the later cemeteries focus on the point where the Trajanic road connecting the harbour to the Tiber reaches the river. Some of the mausolea here also may have been used by the community from Ostia, with funerary cortèges arriving by river. In such a context the probable temples where the road meets the river may have marked the boundary between the worlds of the living and the dead.

Despite this possible shared use of cemeteries, the evidence does suggest that the resident population at Portus was fairly numerous. Residential areas seem to have been concentrated in the southern part of the port, between the *Canale di Comunicazione Trasverso* and the *Episcopio*, in an area covering *c*. 12 ha. The Via Flavia enters the site here, crossing the *Fossa Traiana* over the *Ponte di Matidia*, which was arguably built in the Hadrianic period. This bridge provided access to those working in Portus who would in all probability have lived in the settlement on the Isola Sacra to the south of the *Fossa Traiana*, although its known extent is only *c*. 3 ha. Further high-ranking officials involved in port business may also have been based at Ostia.

FIG. 9.6. General view of the *Palazzo Imperiale* behind the *Terrazza di Traiano* as seen from the southwest. *(Photo: Martin Millett.)*

The growth of Portus as a community distinct from Ostia may be emphasized also by the terminology used to refer to it, although it is only in the later Empire that it came to be known simply as Portus and the cognomen Portuensis came into use (see below, pp. 13–14; Meiggs 1973: 87). Whilst we should not put too much emphasis on this evidence, it is suggestive of changing attitudes to the port. Equally, Bruun (2002: 164–7) has shown how the organization of the *annona* reflects the changing relationship between the two centres. Thus, in the Trajanic period there is evidence for the office of *procurator annonae Ostiae et in Portu*, but, perhaps as a result of a Severan reorganization, the operation at Portus later became autonomous.

Symbols of imperial power are more evident in the Trajanic harbour than in the Claudian harbour. This is possibly because it is later and the evidence is better preserved or, more likely, because of the increased practice of using buildings and monuments to display imperial power by the Trajanic period. The best evidence is provided by the surviving inscriptions that invoke the names of individual emperors (Thylander 1952; Sacco 1984) and the statues and busts of individual emperors of second- and third-century date (Tables 9.2 and 9.3). Equally, as the famous Torlonia relief (Fig. 9.7) now seems most likely to date to the early third century AD, it can perhaps be taken to provide an impression of the opulence of the mid-Imperial harbour (Visconti 1884: no. 430; Boetto 2001b). Nevertheless, the most eloquent statement of Roman power remains the massive scale of engineering involved in the construction of the hexagonal basin and its surrounding facilities. Indeed, the tone of one contemporary panegyric celebrates Trajan's construction of a new canal in terms of altering the work of nature, by saying that he 'let the sea into the shore and moved the shore out to sea', while the port now 'linked far distant peoples by trade so that natural products in any place now seem to belong to all' (**B14**). Our understanding of why Trajan and his architect chose a hexagonal shape for the harbour also suggests that it provided a novel way of enhancing the visible presence

FIG. 9.7. **The so-called Torlonia relief showing a harbour scene at Portus (Visconti 1884: no. 430).** *(Photo: Soprintendenza per i Beni Archeologici di Ostia.)*

of imperial power. This emphasized the ideological associations of the Claudian harbour, and the role of Portus as the monumental gateway to Rome from the empire at large.

This architectural statement would have been obvious to those approaching from either land or sea. Entry into the impressive hexagonal basin and its focus on the temple complex opposite the entrance have been discussed already. The route that connected Portus with the Tiber was equally carefully choreographed, with the road set centrally between the canal and aqueduct. If we are correct in our tentative identification of two features flanking the road near the river as piers that supported an arch similar to the one commemorated in the Torlonia relief (**Fig. 9.7**; Visconti 1884: no. 430), then one can see this acting as a monumental gateway to Portus for those arriving by river from Rome.

NOTES

1. The reading of the archaeological evidence developed here is used in a computer-based virtual reality reconstruction (http://www.arch.soton.ac.uk/portus/) funded by an AHRC Dissemination Grant.
2. We owe this point to Dr Janet DeLaine.

Architecture, Space, and Society in the Roman World: Quotidian Architecture and Individual Space

An edifice august, huge, magnificent not with a hundred columns, but with as many as would support heaven and the gods, were Atlas eased of his burden. The neighbouring palace of the Thunderer [temple of Jupiter on the Capitoline] views it with awe, and the powers rejoice that thou [i.e., Domitian] hast a like abode. Nor wouldst thou hasten to ascend to the great sky; so huge expands the pile, and the reach of the far-flung hall, more unhampered than a plain, embracing beneath its shelter a vast expanse of air, and only lesser than its lord; he fills the house. . . . Libyan mountain and gleaming Ilian stone are rivals there, and much Syenite and Chian and the marble that vies with the grey-green sea; and Luna also, chosen but to bear the pillars' weight. Far upward travels the view; scarce does the tired vision reach the summit, and you would deem it the golden ceiling of the sky. Here when Caesar has bidden the Roman chieftains and the ranks of knighthood recline together at a thousand tables, Ceres herself with robe upgirt and Bacchus might strive to serve them.

The Palatine palace continued as the central official residence of the emperor as long as the emperor remained in Rome, periodically refurbished and expanded, and was always a stunning public showplace. But it is doubtful that its "homey" qualities were ever intended to be considered. Later grand palaces—such as that of Diocletian at Split (Spalato)—took their cue from the Palatine complex and became grand official "residences" constructed for administrative and display purposes more than for domestic appointments or convenience. How the emperors lived in them, or whether they did so any more than was absolutely necessary, we do not know.

APARTMENTS AND APARTMENT BUILDINGS

The forms of domestic architecture other than the palaces, the atrium mansions, and single houses of the aristocrats and well-to-do (or at least the financially comfortable) that must concern us are the abodes available to the rest of the urban population, which were far more modest and for the most part rented rather than owned. Probably the most ubiquitous was also the most humble: the simple dwelling on the floor above a taberna, corresponding in size to the establishment beneath it and usually inhabited by the propietors of

the business. The examples at numbers 1 and 2/3 in Insula 1.x at Pompeii, which we surveyed, are very typical. Other than these shop/dwellings, there were essentially three types of home available in a Roman city, and they seem to have varied a good deal in size and cost.

First are the so-called strip houses, which are usually assumed to have been common although neither Pompeii nor Ostia has produced many examples. These are quite simple, consisting of a property in which a taberna opens onto the street with a stairway on one side to a second storey, often consisting of one or two apartments of varied shapes, and a corridor (much like the fauces of the atrium) opens on the other, which led to a narrow passageway running straight to the rear of the property. Off this passage opened several rooms one after the other and a small courtyard or light well. An example known from Herculaneum is the so-called Casa del Papiro Dipinto at IV.8–9;[31] such apartments resemble nothing so much as the plan of the old-fashioned railroad pullman car. Strip apartments of this kind were sometimes inserted into originally sizeable atrium houses that had been divided up into apartments and/or commercial establishments.

Such reworked houses represent the second type of dwelling available in Roman cities and towns to potential renters of various economic levels. A particularly vivid example is the Casa a Graticcio in Herculaneum, which had been converted through extensive employment of the wattle-and-daub opus craticium denounced by Vitruvius into a complex with a taberna opening onto the street next to the original fauces, a porter's cubbyhole and bedroom opposite it, behind which were an apartment or workshops or a combination of the two lit by three small courtyards. A staircase inserted into the first of these, partially masked by a partition in opus craticium, led to the upper floor which had been divided into two separate residential spaces, one apartment at the rear reached by this staircase, and another facing onto the street reached by its own exterior staircase. The building appears to have been in a state of transition in A.D. 79 and suggests the variety of social classes that could be accommodated in tight spaces in a Roman town. The front upstairs apartment was noticeably more spacious and grand than that behind it, even including a hearth for cooking and a large room that opened onto a balcony. Its second-floor partner was smaller and much more modest, while such accommodation as there was on the ground floor (which is difficult to determine given the condition of the house after the eruption of Vesuvius; all but the porter's sleeping cell may have been in the process of being converted to workshop space at the time of the disaster) was poor and mean.[32] The situation in the Casa a Graticcio is typical of the fate of many substantial atrium houses in the Vesuvian cities and is attested also in Ostia and Rome.

The third type of normal domicile was the *insula* or multiple-unit apartment building. As we have seen, *insula* was the term regularly employed to indicate a city block, but at the same time it appears in both legal texts and inscriptions as the term appropriate to buildings that hold more than one dwelling. The two fourth century A.D. Regionary Catalogues that survive—strange lists of buildings, both famous and humble, in the fourteen regions of Rome during the reign of Constantine—make the problem a great deal more complicated by offering the information that there were either 44,200 or 46,602 *insulae* in the city of Rome at that era, for which gigantic number there is no possible way to find the space within the Aurelianic walls if *insula* here means either a city block or a freestanding apartment building without party walls, as it was defined by Festus and the legal writers.[33] The word may well have had an extremely broad application in the legal texts and in the Regionary Catalogues but leaves us without a proper Latin word for the typical apartment building. Hence, I shall continue to use *insula* occasionally to refer to the multistorey Ostian type of apartment building for convenience' sake—despite having used it previously to refer to a city block—while recognizing that this is a far too limited definition of the term.

Vitruvius knew of the multistorey apartment buildings in Rome by his time and seems distrustful, as well as mildly contemptuous, of them. Nonetheless, it is from his testimony that we must start:[35]

Public statues do not allow a thickness of more than a foot and a half to be used for party walls. But other walls also are put up of the same thickness lest the space be too much narrowed. Now brick walls of a foot and a half—not being two or three bricks thick—cannot sustain more than one storey. Yet with this greatness of the city and the unlimited crowding of citizens, it is necessary to provide very numerous dwellings. Therefore since a level site could not receive such a multitude to dwell in the city, circumstances themselves have compelled the resort to raising the height of buildings. And so by means of stone pillars, walls of burnt [baked or kiln-dried] brick, party walls of rubble [and concrete], towers [high buildings] have been raised, and these being joined together by frequent board floors produce upper stories [of apartments] with fine views over the city to the utmost advantage. Therefore walls are raised to a great height through various stories, and the Roman people has excellent dwellings without hindrance.

Despite the doubts he expresses, Vitruvius has here encapsulated the nature of the Roman apartment building and the examples excavated at Ostia confirm his basic description but refine the details. Of course, the evidence from Ostia is almost all a good deal later than Vitruvius's description and so shows refinements and developments not known to him.

At Ostia the basic plan of a high-rise building of three to five stories with apartments of ever decreasing size and cost as one proceeded higher was subject to a variety of modifications of plan. The two most useful ways of categorizing the *insulae* would divide them into classes based, first, on the number and disposition of the shops (single row, two rows back to back, three or four rows grouped around a courtyard, shops mingled with apartments on the ground floor) or, second, on the uses to which the ground floors of the various *insulae* were put (shops, apartments, manufactories, workrooms).[36] To take one Ostian example as typical, though by no means universal, may help to make the use of space in the *insula* clearer. The Casa di Diana (I.iii.3) faces onto the via di Diana east of the Capitolium temple and northeast of the Forum (fig. 6.3).

On the ground floor, *tabernae* opened onto the street on two sides of the building (4, 6, 8–11, 15, 16), two of them with a second room each behind the first (5, 7). The residential area of the apart-

to permit internal access only) and at least one more (26) for internal access only. On the second floor, which has been less thoroughly studied and is less well preserved, the sets of rooms seem clearly to have been grouped into apartment units of various sizes: we can be fairly certain that two apartments facing onto the via di Diana and lighted by windows onto it were of three (12, 13, 15) and two (14 and successor) rooms in size, respectively. The forms of the apartments along the west side of the second floor are not known but the rooms from which they were made up were rectangles of more or less similar size with street windows. What appears to be a spacious single room (8) at the north end with three openings onto the light coming in from the courtyard was in fact not space to be used on the second floor at all; it was rather the upper part of a large two-storey room. The apartment on the northeast side of the second floor (6, 7) seems to have been a long narrow set of rooms opening off a straight corridor that led to the main room of the apartment at the back, in fact one type of *cenaculum medianum*.[37] We do not know anything of the building above the second storey.

Several points about the uses of space may be raised from looking at this apartment building. First, it must be noted that the apartments vary a good deal both in size and in availability of light. Presumably the most expensive ones were on the ground floor, closest to both the water cistern (which itself was a later addition to the apartment house, not part of its original amenities) and the latrine. But clearly the combination of rooms into particular apartments could be changed as circumstances and finances dictated (e.g., the periodic reworkings that seem to have taken place in 23, 24, and 25, or between 30 and 5 and 7). On the second floor, the most pleasant of the apartments must have been rooms 12, 13, and 15, although the exact relationship of 12 to 13 and 15 as well as to 14 and successor is completely unclear and could have changed over time (indeed, 13, 15, and the successor to 14 might have shared access to 12). The 6 and 7 complex of four small and one large room could well have been rented out to more than one family, or to a large extended kin group. The Casa di Diana *insula* is remarkable for having, at least in one of its later incarnations, provided a water cistern and a latrine (it is reported that evidence for an earlier

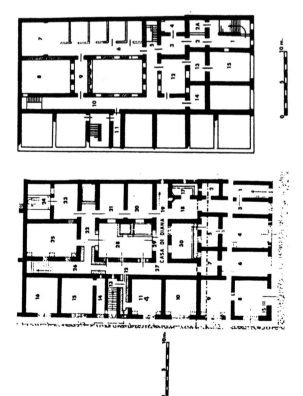

Figure 6.3 Ostia: Casa di Diana. [Packer (1971) plans 2 & 3; reproduced by permission of the author]

ment building was entered through *fauces*, the primary one (3) on via di Diana and secondary ones (12/13, subsequently blocked up, and 19) among the side street shops. Entering from via di Diana the resident or visitor encountered a porter's lodge (2) and a communal latrine (17) before passing through a vestibule (18) and reaching the central courtyard (28) which contained a cistern to provide water for the inhabitants. The courtyard was surrounded by a corridor (22, 26, 27) and several sets of rooms, some independent (20, 21), others interconnected, including one group of three (23, 24, 25) from which the largest room (25) was later blocked off (perhaps when 24 was altered to contain a Mithraeum at some point), and another (30) that was at some time connected with the back rooms of the two via di Diana shops (5, 7) but had been converted, it would appear, into a stable.

Access to the second floor was by staircases, two opening onto the surrounding streets (1 and 13, though 13 was later blocked off

angle and its gardens were completely geometrically regular. The planning of proportions and light, of open spaces and entrances, was remarkable for its geometrical sophistication in the central block of apartments, a plan of one section of which is highly revealing (fig. 6.4).

A look at the plan shows that these apartments had some luxurious appointments, as well as elaborate geometrical layout, incorporated into them. The *medianum* seems to have been two stories high as were the two rooms at either of its ends (the smaller one perhaps a dining room [*triclinium*], the larger an *oecus* or some sort of substitute for a *tablinum*). All three spaces were lit by two rows of windows, placed one above the other. The putative bedrooms (*cubicula*) opening off the *medianum* were usually only one storey high, which allowed additional *cubicula* to be incorporated into the second storey, which was reached by a private internal staircase. This generic apartment plan, a development of the so-called *casette-tipo* plan, was repeated throughout the remarkably carefully planned and precisely executed complex.[38]

In most, probably all, Roman *insulae*, the *medianum* was jointly held common space within the apartment. This is shown by the famous legal example commented upon by Ulpian that states that if a number of people inhabit the same apartment and some damage is done by anything that has been tossed or poured into the street from a window, they can all be sued for damages as a group (*in solidum*) since it would be impossible to determine who did the evil deed. If, however, a number of persons share the apartment but inhabit separate sections of it, a suit can only be brought against the person who inhabited that part of the apartment from which the object was tossed or liquid was poured. Another example states that if someone rents an apartment to several people and keeps a part of the space for himself, everyone including the owner is responsible for damage done, and although it is possible to start proceedings against one individual in the apartment if the object or liquid came from his or her private window, if it was thrown or poured from the windows of the *medianum*, then everyone living in the apartment is regarded as equally liable.[39] These passages attest not only to the nature of the rentals of apartments in Rome, a subject upon which

pre-cistern fountain has been found, but this has not been published and so was presumably quite a desirable building in which to live both as originally designed and even more so after its amenities were substantially improved. The multiplicity of staircases also attests to the convenience of the tenants being of concern to designer and landlord.

The *cenaculum medianum*, possibly exemplified in the Casa di Diana by apartment 6, 7 on the second floor, was the most common form of apartment in Ostia's *insulae*. The term *cenaculum* occurs in the legal writers of the *Digest* as the term for the spaces into which an *insula* was divided, and is regularly so defined. Hence, it is presumably the general term for an "apartment." The designation *medianum* refers to a particular and very common design of *cenaculum*. Other clearer examples include, especially, the carefully geometrically planned and balanced apartments of the Garden Apartments complex, those in the Casa dei Dipinti, the Casa di via della Fontana, and the Casete tipo complex. Such apartments consisted of a series of small rooms (*cubicula*) that opened off a long hallway or room (*medianum*) that ran along one outer wall and was pierced by a series of windows that provided the main light source for the entire apartment; at one or both ends there was a larger room (*exedra*). Of those examples, the most remarkable are the Garden Apartments, one of the most highly developed apartment complexes known to us from the Roman world.

The Garden Apartments (located at III.ix.13–20) are perhaps the clearest example known to us of "drawing board" or "blueprint" construction in Roman architecture. Built after the Hadrianic reorganization of Ostia, this complex makes highly inventive use of the irregular space available to its builder by reducing what was in essence a very rough trapezoid of land into a development of two long rectangular blocks divided up into four rigidly symmetrical apartments on the ground floor, which looked out onto gardens that filled out the uncouth remaining space of the open area. Thus they had no commercial frontage whatsoever and are supposed to have been relatively "high rent" properties. The odd shape of the plot was disguised by the varying widths and depths of the structures that were run up around the gardens, while the inner rect-

there has been much useful study, but to the nature of communal space within them—which in turn clearly implies that apartments did not have to be rented out solely to related families and kinship units—but that the owner or his rental agent had a fair amount of flexibility in determining to whom they would rent. Other requirements and niceties of renting an apartment, as well as the overall nature of the Roman rental market, are attested in the legal sources in substantial if sometimes confusing detail.[40]

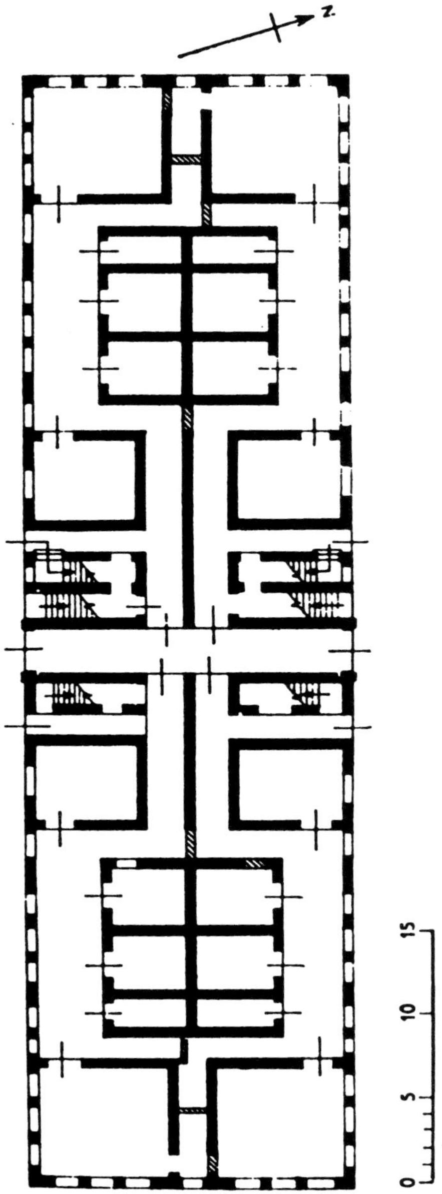

With the evidence of Ostia and of the legal writers available, it is time to consider the situation in Rome itself. Vitruvius has already provided the essential evidence that Rome was turning increasingly into a city of high-rise apartment buildings by the 20s B.C., but examples from archaeology are relatively few. *Insulae* at Rome are known (1) on the slope of the Capitoline Hill just to the left of the staircase that leads to S. Maria in Aracoeli, (2) incorporated into the Aurelianic Walls at Porta S. Lorenzo, (3) built into the church of SS. Giovanni e Paolo, (4) beneath the modern Galleria Colonna on via del Corso, and (5) on via Giulio Romano, though none is in any way complete. Those beneath Galleria Colonna have yielded the most extensive ground plan.

In general *insulae* at Rome seem to confirm the evidence from Ostia since they contain shops with small apartments immediately above, larger apartments lit by rows of windows, probably of the *medianum* type, and perhaps even examples that can be read as "strip" apartments, but the evidence to be recovered from archaeological excavation in these mundane buildings in so busy and vigorous a modern city is inevitably limited.[41] Two other sources of information more valuable in determining the urban spaces available to Roman apartment dwellers in antiquity are the literary record, especially the letters of Seneca and the poetry of Martial and Juvenal, and the fragments of the Severan marble plan that show the streets and apartment complexes of Rome shortly after A.D. 200. The fragments of the Severan map reveal tremendous diversity

Figure 6.4 Ostia: Plan of the ground floor of the central block of apartments in the Garden Apartments complex. [Pavolini (1983) p. 157; reproduced by permission of Gius. Laterza & Figli, S.p.a.].

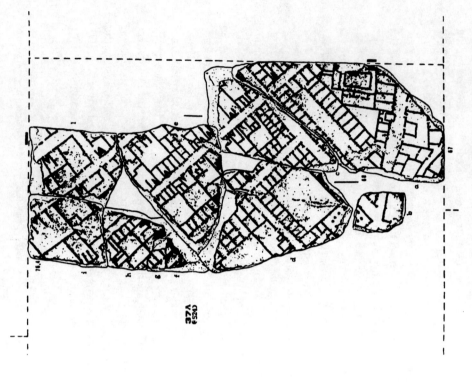

Figure 6.5 Rome: Residential quarter on the Janiculum as shown on the Marble Plan. [Gros & Torelli (1988) p. 205, fig. 92; reproduced by permission of Gius. Laterza & Figli, S.p.a.]

among the various habitations they show, reminiscent of a mixing together of Pompeii and Ostia and expanded to a much larger scale. The fragments confirm the information provided by the Regionary Catalogues that *insulae* were far more numerous than atrium-type houses in the city, and they further reveal vast numbers of *tabernae* of every sort along the street frontages. The main areas of habitation shown on the remaining fragments are a reasonably representative sample of residential quarters of the city: the Esquiline east of the Porticus Liviae along the clivus Suburanus, the streets of houses and shops on the Janiculum (fig. 6.5), and the area on the Viminal along the vicus Patricius.

All three reveal a schematic diagram of the urban texture of Rome at the beginning of the third century A.D. that emphasizes the importance of *insula* and *taberna*, apartment buildings and shopfronts, interspersed apparently at random with the larger single houses of the wealthy (or ones that had been subdivided into apartments; the scale of the plan does not permit such fine distinctions to be observed). This is the picture we would have expected from Ostia and, secondarily, Pompeii and Herculaneum, and it is precisely the picture that the marble plan confirms.[42]

From the archaeological evidence, we can turn to the testimony of Romans who lived in the *insulae* of the Imperial city. Two complaints, among many, seem to be overwhelmingly common: the flimsiness and combustibility of the apartment buildings, and the noise and innumerable inconveniences that had to be endured by those living in them.[43] The poorer the apartment dweller, the higher in the structure he had to live (the opposite of a situation frequent in our own time when top-floor apartments are often the largest and most expensive) and the flimsier its construction was likely to be. Perhaps Juvenal, in his well-known Third Satire, paints the most vivid picture of life in and around the *insulae* of Imperial Rome:[44]

Who at cool Praeneste, or at Volsinii amid its leafy hills, was ever afraid of his house tumbling down? Who in modest Gabii, or on the sloping heights of Tivoli? But here we inhabit a city propped up for the most part by slender flute-players: for that is how the bailiff patches up the cracks in the old wall, bidding the inmates sleep at ease under a roof ready to

tumble about their ears. No, no, I must live where there are no fires, no nightly alarms. Ucalegon below is already shouting for water and shifting his chattels; smoke is pouring out of your third floor attic above, but you know nothing of it; for if the alarm begins in the ground floor, the last man to burn will be he who has nothing to shelter him from the rain but the tiles, where the gentle doves lay their eggs. . . . If you can tear yourself away from the games of the Circus, you can buy an excellent house at Sora, or Fabrateria or Frusino, for what you now pay in Rome to rent a dark garret for one year. . . . Most sick people here in Rome perish for want of sleep, the illness itself having been produced by food lying undigested on a fevered stomach. For what sleep is possible in a lodging? Who but the wealthy get sleep in Rome? There lies the root of the disorder. The crossing of wagons in the narrow winding streets, the slanging of drovers when brought to a stand, would make sleep impossible for a Drusus—or a sea calf. When the rich man has a call of social duty, the mob makes way for him as he is borne swiftly over their heads in a huge Liburnian car. He writes or reads or sleeps as he goes along, for the closed window of the litter induces slumber. Yet he will arrive before us; hurry as we may, we are blocked by a surging crowd in front, and by a dense mass of people pressing in on us from behind: one man digs an elbow into me, another a sedan-pole; one bangs a beam, another a wine cask, against my head. My legs are be-plastered with mud; huge feet trample on me from every side, and a soldier plants his hobnails firmly on my toe. . . . And now regard the different and diverse perils of the night. See what a height it is to that towering roof from which a potsherd comes crack upon my head every time that some broken or leaky vessel is pitched out of the window! See with what a smash it strikes and dints the pavement! There's death in every open window as you pass along at night; you may well be deemed a fool, improvident of sudden accident, if you go out to dinner without having made your will.

Of course, Juvenal's picture is a conscious exaggeration for his own satirical purposes, but the vivid detail of life at the top of an *insula* and the innumerable difficulties involved probably rang all too true to those who might have heard it in Juvenal's own time and who lived in apartment buildings, even the best accommodations in the best buildings. With the sarcasm and cynicism removed, what Juvenal has painted is a clear and convincing picture of the usual inconveniences and dangers of life in a heavily populated city and in the urban texture of the *insula*, seen both as apartment building and as city block.

VILLA AND FARM

Outside the cities and towns, rural private architecture was determined almost entirely by function. Rural habitations ranged from

316